So Many Shoes, So Little Money

A Girl's Guide to Finance

LISA SERWIN

ISBN: 1-4392-3121-4
ISBN-13: 9781439231210

Visit www.booksurge.com to order additional copies.

Dedication

To Brad—for everything

--

Acknowledgements

Writing a book really does require a lot of shoes. I want to thank my parents, Fred and Susan Salenger, for their unwavering support in everything I do; my editor, Nancy Hardin, for her wonderful advice; Elizabeth Lyon and Polly Bowman for their suggestions and encouragement; my husband, Brad, for everything; and my sister and friends for their endless copy reading, support, editorial skills and smashing sense of style: Dr. Jill Kane, Khaia Brogan, Fiona Campbell, Juliana Nelson, Rita Ravindra, Kim Sinatra, Melissa Stewart, Rebecca Swank and Wendi Webster. Without them, this book would be a lot less informative and fashionable.

Table of Contents

Author Preface

Learning about finance does not have to put you to sleep. Watch—I'll jolt you awake faster than a double espresso would with just three words: Shopping, shopping, shopping. Okay, so it was one word three times, but I got your attention, didn't I? Finance is important, but shopping is critical.

"Yes, but shopping isn't finance," you say. Yes, it is. Here's how: Shopping requires money, and money requires finance. So if you understand finance, you'll understand money, and understanding money allows you to shop, thereby fulfilling your insatiable need for that Louis Vuitton bag.

Dressing with style takes patience, planning, and strategy. So does managing your money. Dressing with style on a budget takes even *more* patience, planning, and strategy. Knowing your income, figuring out how much you can spend, and how much to save, all require strategy. Knowing whether you can afford the current "it" bag, and how to still look good if you can't, are an integral part of understanding and managing your finances. Of course you care about more than just shopping for the latest fashions. That's a given. But shopping provides a great framework within which to talk about money and finance in general.

Finance, and therefore money, often gets a bad rap. Women who like money and want more of it are too often considered ambitious, greedy, or gold diggers. However, having money can be a truly enjoyable—even life changing— experience. At its best, money is about freedom and choices, about having options and opportunities. It's about being able to live the life you want to live in the way you want to live it. Money allows you to travel, to go to school, or to work at something that offers you full satisfaction, regardless of compensation, instead of being stuck in a job you hate just to pay the bills. Money gives you the freedom to choose whether to buy that Prada bag or the Gucci boots or, in a perfect world, *both*. Money allows you to be self-sufficient, with the confidence that comes with being independent and the freedom to make life choices that are right for you. It doesn't guarantee all this, but it certainly ups the odds. It's a means to an end we all aspire to.

So knowing how to manage your money is vital. There are a lot of decisions you will make over the years (student loans, buying a car, buying a house, how many pairs of shoes you can own without being obscene) that will rely on your having a basic understanding of your personal finances. Money can be cheap or expensive depending on what you know about how to use it. For example, if you charge those Manolo Blahnik shoes—the ones you know perfectly well you can't afford—to your credit card and don't pay the bill in full when it arrives in the mail, the shoes become a lot more expensive than the original number that was on the price tag because of the interest the credit company charges.

Like many women, I grew up thinking I was good at shopping but bad with numbers and math. Shopping is inherently more fun than math, but since shopping requires math, I'm not sure why I felt this way or why so many other women feel this way today. Although this attitude is changing, historically, girls weren't supposed to like or excel at figures and, as a result, were rarely encouraged to take math classes. There were also women who were hard put to discern any practical applications for math, so why bother? For me, it was a combination of the above. Whatever the reasons, I simply didn't enjoy it and avoided it whenever possible.

In college, I majored in history so I could read and write instead of add and subtract. But no matter how hard I tried, I couldn't seem to entirely get around dealing with numbers. They were everywhere. For a history major, there were dates to memorize and population statistics and economic cycles to grasp. I had to concede that since the world was turning out to be full of numbers, I should make an effort to understand them better. So I took a deep breath, made a big leap, and decided to sign up for a beginning accounting class.

I'm glad I did. Our final exam required us to create and run a small business. I couldn't come up with what kind of business to start so I fell back on something familiar—shopping. I built a virtual retail store, with make-believe inventory and make-believe customers. Our exam package even had tiny pretend checks for us to write. I admit to being thrilled when my fake business succeeded. I was even more pleased when I realized that, in launching a successful store simply in order to get an "A" in the class, I had overcome one of my biggest *bêtes noires*—numbers and math—while doing a lot of imaginary shopping and having all kinds of fun in the process.

After I graduated from college, I still didn't know what I wanted to be or how I wanted to earn a living. Since my first accounting class had gone so well, and since I had come to realize math and numbers were important in life, I decided to take a few more accounting classes and found I really enjoyed them. I made another leap, this one gigantic, and enrolled in business school, eventually acquiring a master's degree in business administration.

One of the central things I learned in business school was that I already possessed the math skills I needed to learn finance. I didn't have to be a whiz with numbers. Since I was a canny shopper, I had the basics. Trust me: To manage your money effectively, you really don't need to have studied advanced calculus or quantum physics. You only need addition and subtraction. Okay, multiplication and division help, as do fractions and percents, but that's really it. I will prove this to you with a pop quiz that I suspect you'll pass with ease:

■ Question 1: You have one hundred dollars. That fabulous scarf in the window, which could double as a belt, costs fifty dollars. Can you buy it in two colors?

■ Question 2: You have one hundred dollars. You see *très chic* cuffs that cost thirty-nine dollars each. Three of them together are terrific. They are 15 percent off. Can you get all three?

If you answered yes to both these questions then congratulations—you possess the math required to understand finance and manage your money. If you answered no, but it was because you figured in taxes, then again, congratulations—you also passed. If you did not remember to add in the taxes, then make a note to remember next time. If you answered no because you really didn't know, then:

■ The two scarves equal one hundred dollars (50 plus 50 equals 100)

■ The three cuffs equal 117 dollars (39 plus 39 plus 39); 15 percent of 117 dollars equals $17.55; 117 dollars minus $17.55 equals $99.45.

Which do you choose—the scarves or the cuffs? That, I can't help you with—it depends on how you decide to accessorize!

The table below will further demonstrate to you that you already know the necessary math:

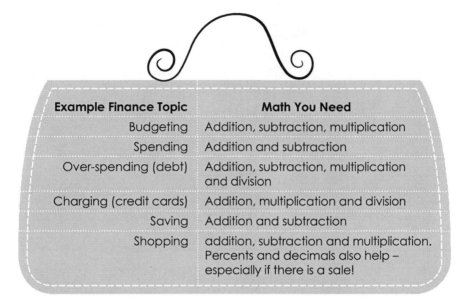

Example Finance Topic	Math You Need
Budgeting	Addition, subtraction, multiplication
Spending	Addition and subtraction
Over-spending (debt)	Addition, subtraction, multiplication and division
Charging (credit cards)	Addition, multiplication and division
Saving	Addition and subtraction
Shopping	addition, subtraction and multiplication. Percents and decimals also help – especially if there is a sale!

Notice that algebra is not listed; geometry is nowhere in sight (although one way to save money is to *angle* around the outer *perimeters* of the shoe department); trigonometry—forget it; calculus—don't need it. So take a deep breath and keep reading. You can do this.

The second thing I learned is: Shopping provides you with all of the tools you need to manage your money. When you shop, you make the same kinds of decisions you make when you manage your finances: What works for you and what doesn't, whether you can afford whatever it is, and how you are going to pay for it. Who would have thought shopping could be so educational? And if you begin to think about your personal finances in terms of shopping, then what might have felt daunting becomes manageable, easy, and, dare I say, even fun.

I cover a lot of ground in the chapters that follow. Think of the book as a closet filled with a variety of subjects instead of clothes and shoes. As is the case with any well-stocked closet, you can pick and choose what you need from it whenever you want, then keep referring back to it as necessary. Key terms have been highlighted in bold face so you will know when you are being introduced to a new word or definition. There is a summary at the end of each chapter called "Organize Your Financial Closet" that highlights the main ideas in the chapter and offers step-by-step ways of applying the material covered. A few chapters also have additional material after the summary. I've also included a glossary and a list of resources at the end of the book.

• • •

Chapter 1: Budget Basics
What's In Your Closet?
(And What's Missing?)

We've all had those mornings. You find yourself staring blankly into your closet trying to figure out what to wear. While you're repeating "I have nothing to wear" over and over in your head like a mantra, suddenly your eyes fall upon *those* pants, the ones you always feel fantastic wearing, the ones that make your rear look truly miniscule. As you grab them, you realize that they will look perfect with a little t-shirt, maybe those cute flats, and your favorite shoulder bag. Lo and behold you're dressed and looking fabulous! All it took was a place to start.

Money can be like those mornings, in that it can seem very daunting when all you need is a place to start. After all, how do you know how much you can spend if you don't even know what you have? So where does one begin, you ask. One begins by

> **⤳FASHIONISTA FACT⤳**
> The word "fashionista" was coined by Stephen Fried in *Thing of Beauty*, his 1993 biography of the supermodel Gia, to describe a designer, promoter, or arbiter of the latest fashions. Fashionista has since been broadened to "one who follows fashion" though some mean-spirited folks use it to mean "clotheshorse." In 2007, Larry Kudlow, an economist, used "recessionista" to describe "a style maven on a budget" but it developed a fierce competitor in "frugalista," coined by Natalie McNeal in her *Miami Herald* blog *The Frugalista Files*. *The New York Times* named "frugalista" as its choice for the 2008 word of the year.

making a budget. Why? Because making a budget is all about living within your means, knowing you're on top of things, in control. Regardless of how much or—more to the point—how little money you have, if you live within your means, you'll still have choices. Maybe not as many choices as you would like, but definitely choices.

So let's start with your income. Your income consists of what you receive from a paycheck or allowance or maybe tips, along with what you receive from your investments. (Later we'll go over the taxes that are deducted, or not, from what you're paid.) Write down what you receive each month, along with its source. The final total should be what your checks and cash add up to, after items like taxes, insurance, and your 401K plan are taken out.

Next, write down how much you spend and what you spend it on. You don't know? Not to worry. Many women—and men too—are unaware of where a lot of their money goes. If I asked you how much you paid for this morning's iced mocha and muffin would you know, exactly? My guess is no. But you will see how the little things we buy without even thinking about it really add up. (Incidentally, if you didn't know the price of that iced mocha and muffin, chances are you do know the num-

> ∾**FASHIONISTA FACT**∾
> Our ability to count our calories but not our money is good for our hips, but not for our finances. By the way, the iced mocha has 320 calories (Starbucks, Grande, 2 percent milk and whipped cream) and there are approximately 420 calories in the muffin (if blueberry and depending on where you live—different Starbucks buy their pastries from different places).

ber of calories they add up to. Women are often better at counting calories than their money.)

Just as you should know how to put an outfit together in order to spare yourself the embarrassment of turning up in a fashion don't, so should you know where and how much you're spending to avoid the embarrassments of a *financial* don't, such as spending more than you have. To get you started figuring all this out, I've made the following list of items on which you are likely spending money almost every month:

- Rent or mortgage
- Food
- Laundry
- Medical expenses
- Clothes, shoes, and bags!
- Beauty products (hair, face, body, and nails)
- Personal services (hair cut, color, manicure/pedicure, waxing)
- Student loans
- Social activities (movies, restaurants, the gym)
- Caffeine
- Cell phone
- Utilities
- Internet (including downloads)
- Car payments
- Savings

Notice how the list of items we spend our money on is longer than the list of money sources? Sad truth—it always seems to be that way, no matter how much you earn.

"But wait," you protest, "except for basic stuff like rent and car payments and my student loan, a lot of things you've listed are different every month." Don't despair. Just as it takes time and effort, along with a little planning, to come up with the perfect outfit, it can take some time and effort to figure out your average expenses. But it is do-able. A good way to start is to ask for receipts for *every single* thing you buy. When you order your macchiato, get the receipt. When you buy your lunch, get the receipt. When you pay the phone bill, keep the receipt. Throw all the receipts you collect into one place— a drawer or basket, it doesn't matter as long as they're all in one place. Do this for one month, preferably a fairly typical one. At the end of that month, take them all out and sort them into piles: Food, utility bills, clothes—use and build on the categories I listed or create your own. Just by sorting, you can start to see exactly where your money is going. It is okay to not sort them; I would rather you do the exercise than not do it. Then, add up all the receipts. Yes, *all* of them, even the one for those earrings you just bought and are trying to dismiss as a one time thing and therefore irrelevant. No cheating.

Now, take the total of the money that came in that month and then total the money you spent. Subtract the money you spent from the money you brought in, and voila! You just made your first budget. In so doing, you figured out something really essential: Whether or not you have any money left over, which is the number one indicator of whether or not you are over-spending. And if you need help visualizing what a budget looks like, there are sample budgets at the end of this chapter that will give you an idea.

Creating a budget is the first and most important step you can take toward managing your money and creating a sound financial plan. Only by knowing what you have (and what you don't have) can you figure out the next step—whether you can save, spend, or should cut costs.

I bet many of you thought budgets were really complicated to put together, but you have already completed one, and you're only on page 5. There is one more thing you have to do, though: Multiply by twelve. Since you only wrote down what you made and spent for one month, you must multiply both totals by twelve to arrive at an approximate budget for a whole year.

In reality, the amounts you spend will fluctuate from month to month. But creating an approximate budget will give you a pretty good idea of what you spend every month. In the next chapter we will add some complications if you'd like to refine your budget, but this will give you a good start.

Sample Monthly Budget

	EXAMPLE 1: IN GIRL		EXAMPLE 2: OUT GIRL	
Money In				
Paycheck	$	3,000	$	1,500
Tips	$	-	$	500
Parents	$	500	$	500
Sub-total	$	3,500	$	2,500
Money Out				
Rent or mortgage	$	1,000	$	1,000
Food	$	400	$	400
Laundry	$	25	$	25
Medical expenses	$	50	$	50
Clothes, shoes and bags!	$	200	$	250
Beauty products	$	100	$	100
Personal services	$	100	$	150
Student loans	$	-	$	200
Social activities	$	400	$	300
Caffeine	$	60	$	40
Cell phone	$	110	$	110
Utilities	$	75	$	75
Internet	$	25	$	25
Car payments	$	300	$	300
Savings	$	100	$	-
Sub-total	$	2,945	$	3,025
Left Over	$	555	$	-525

Since "Out Girl" has spent 525 dollars more this month than she has, next month she must spend less on clothes, or get a roommate, or find some other place to cut costs. No, starvation is not an option! Anorexia looks pretty on no one, and size 27 jeans cost the same as size 31 jeans so smaller sizes do not help you save money on clothes.

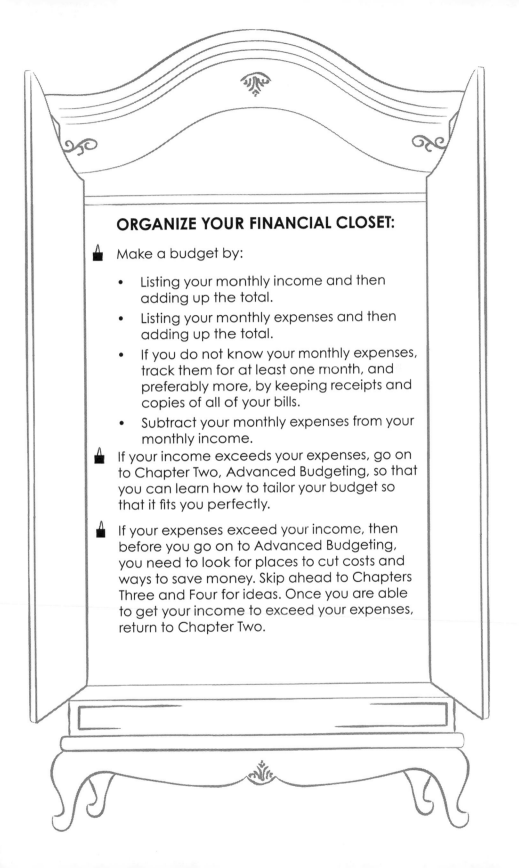

ORGANIZE YOUR FINANCIAL CLOSET:

- Make a budget by:

    - Listing your monthly income and then adding up the total.
    - Listing your monthly expenses and then adding up the total.
    - If you do not know your monthly expenses, track them for at least one month, and preferably more, by keeping receipts and copies of all of your bills.
    - Subtract your monthly expenses from your monthly income.

- If your income exceeds your expenses, go on to Chapter Two, Advanced Budgeting, so that you can learn how to tailor your budget so that it fits you perfectly.

- If your expenses exceed your income, then before you go on to Advanced Budgeting, you need to look for places to cut costs and ways to save money. Skip ahead to Chapters Three and Four for ideas. Once you are able to get your income to exceed your expenses, return to Chapter Two.

WHAT A GIRL WANTS: CHOCOLATE

If making a budget has stressed you out, or if you feel you deserve a reward for drawing up your first budget, know that while shopping doesn't deliver each and every time, chocolate *always* does. So give this treat a try:

One package No Pudge Fat Free Brownie mix™

One small container fat-free vanilla yogurt

Follow the directions.

Bake.

Eat.

The best part: You didn't even blow your diet—unless of course you substituted your favorite ice cream and added a little bit of hot fudge on top.

If brownies aren't your thing, feel free to substitute whatever is.

∽FASHIONISTA FACT∽

Wallis Simpson, the American divorcee for whom King Edward VIII gave up the throne of Great Britain and Ireland, is often credited with originating the saying "You can never be too rich or too thin." However, she was wrong. You actually can be too thin.

• • •

Chapter 2: Advanced Budgeting
Tailor Made (For a Perfect Fit)

It's a constant struggle, a closet full of clothes that all too often offers nothing to wear. The pants you altered for heels, before you acquired a short boyfriend, you now want to wear with flats. The never-go-out-of-style jacket you had to have is now so last season. And the "fill in your own blank" splurge you rationalized by dividing the purchase price by 365 (the number of days you swore you would wear it) no longer looks as good on you as it once did and hasn't been worn in weeks. It's okay, it's a time-honored tradition—we are all guilty of it. Just think of it as proof that division can be your friend. What's a girl to do? Take the item you've fallen out of love with to a tailor and have it re-worked and re-fitted. It's amazing what a bit of tweaking can do. (Although on shoes and bags—not so much, so proceed with caution when splurging on those.)

Budgeting is the same. In Chapter One, we made it easy: One size fits all, one month's worth of income and expenses multiplied by twelve. But as you know, one size never fits all, and is rarely stylish. Elastic bands are fashion's enemy, except during pregnancy. The same is true for budgets: Too much elasticity and you're back where you started. You'll want to alter yours to ensure a perfect fit. This chapter suggests some of the steps you can take, and changes you can make, so your budget fits you to perfection.

It's not *what* you wear—it's *how* you wear it.

It's not what you budget—it's how you utilize it. Attitude is everything. Most budgets fail because they are seen as a restraint as in the plaintive, "It's not in my budget." Instead, start thinking of a budget as a way to help you achieve your life's goals and dreams. A budget doesn't tell you what you can't do, it tells you what you can do. There, isn't that more palatable already?

I haven't expounded on living within your means, which is much more important than the amount of money you have. Whoever you are, no matter how much money you make, more than likely, you'll never have quite enough. Why? Because as your income goes up, so do your expenses. *We all want more than we can afford*. With more money, your tastes upgrade—it's inevitable and normal. You'll want Manolo Blahnik, not Designer Shoe Warehouse, you'll want champagne, not two buck chuck, and you'll want a house with a yard instead of that "cozy" little apartment. The beauty of budgeting is that it tells you what your means are—and means are different for everyone.

Goals and dreams

For a budget to succeed, it helps to have goals. Goals can be short- or long-term, large or small. In fact, it's good to have goals for both. So you're coveting [you fill in the blank].

Whether [blank] is a new car or an expensive cashmere sweater, make use of your budget to save for it.

Set aside a certain amount each month so you can eventually afford it. However, if the amount puts you over your monthly spending allowance, be sure to compensate elsewhere in your budget.

Track your actual spending

The only way to find out if your budget is actually working is to track your spending against what you had planned to spend. How do you do this? Continue to keep those receipts. At the end of every month, add up what money you actually made, what money you actually spent, and what you have left over. Then compare it to what you planned when you made up your budget. If you spent more than you expected, spend less next month. If you spent less, think about putting the surplus money into a savings account.

Whatever initial budget you made, it is guaranteed to need tweaking—or "tailoring," if you will—especially if

> **~FASHIONISTA FACT~**
>
> When buying cashmere, especially expensive cashmere, pay for as many "plys" as you can afford. Two- or three-ply cashmere is sturdier than one-ply, and it will last longer and pill less, so it will save you money in the long run. Be sure to hand-wash cashmere with mild soap or baby shampoo. By not dry cleaning, you will save money and avoid chemicals that can ruin the fibers. After rinsing, lay the garment flat on a towel, using a second towel to press the water out. Then, on a third towel, shape it and let it air dry; do not hang it up to dry - wet or dry hanging ruins a sweater's shape. Sweaters should always be stored folded flat.

it's your first one. You might even find that you've forgotten to budget for entire categories of things you spend money on. Don't give up; just keep adjusting until it fits you perfectly.

Tracking what you actually spend will help you find out what changes you need to make. Whatever the problems, you can adjust your budget to account for them. The point is to create a realistic budget that you will stick with and use long-term.

Once you have achieved a comfort level with making and using a budget, try finalize it and then leave it alone; no more adjustments. If you've done it correctly, your budget should now be capable of signaling when you go off course and need to modify your behavior. For example, if you constantly spend more than budgeted on beauty products, take a good look at what you are buying. Are there cheaper alternatives? Can you do with fewer items? If not, where else can you cut down to compensate for that 300 dollar T3 Bespoke Tourmaline blow dryer?

> **∽FASHIONISTA FACT∽**
> According to a YWCA Report on the consequences of America's beauty obsession, the average woman in the United States spends 100 dollars per month, or 1,200 dollars per year—a total of seven billion spent annually—on cosmetic and beauty products.

Life is in the details

Accessories complete an outfit. As your budgeting expertise increases, you can start to accessorize your budget by adding more details to it. For example, you might want to expand the categories you are tracking by adding new ones, or by breaking down the ones you already have into smaller sections. In our example budget from Chapter One, you could add Beauty (hair, nails, and products) as one new category, or, if you wanted to dig deeper into your spending, you could track hair, nails, and products separately, as three different categories.

Just like fashion, life and finances are seasonal

Just as the seasons come and go, requiring different clothing, you don't expect every month of your financial year to be the same either. If you work on commission, some months might typically be busier than others (holidays at restaurants or retail stores, for example). At some point, you might get a bonus or a raise. Certain bills remain the same every month or change with advance notice (as in your rent will be raised on May 1st); others fluctuate (utilities); and still others you can control, first by deciding whether or not to shop and then by shopping for the best price and by deciding when and how to pay the bill (as in insurance, which you can pay all at once or, for a small surcharge, monthly or quarterly).

If you lay out your budget month by month, instead of just looking at one month and multiplying by twelve as we did in Chapter One, you might be able to match your income and your spending more effectively. For example, if you know you will earn more income in December, but that you will also spend more (you are so good to your friends), plan ahead by perhaps paying at least one installment of one insurance company's bill in monthly or quarterly payments instead of all at once.

Only three things are certain: Death, taxes, and the fact that black is slimming

You can increase or decrease the size of your paycheck, and therefore your take-home pay, depending on how you decide to declare the amount of federal, state, and local taxes that are deducted from each check. The more deductions you take, the less money your employer subtracts from your paycheck. However, you may be simply pushing your tax payments into April of the following year, so weigh the advantages and disadvantages. With careful planning, you can also reduce what you owe. Chapter 15 delves into taxes and how to minimize them.

Pencil and paper are fine

I encourage you to create your first budget by hand. By starting from scratch, you will obtain a good feel and understanding of how budgeting works. This will stand you in good stead when you graduate to an automated program and help you to use it quickly and effectively. However, if you're not up for that, there are financial programs and free websites that will help you build a budget and then refine and analyze it. These programs already have categories laid out and they complete the math for you, including comparing your actual spending to the budget you've created. And often you can download your financial information automatically (checks, deposits, and credit card transactions, for example), making tracking your budget easy and painless.

One of the reasons to use these automated programs is that they offer pie, and who doesn't like pie? (I know, first brownies, now pie—bear with me.) Most automated budget programs will create pie charts for you, and pie charts can help you see where you are spending your money in a quick, color-coded snapshot. They can illustrate spending in all sorts of ways, showing, for example, dollar amounts, or percentages, or both. They are especially good if you feel you are not good with numbers or if you are a more visual person. For some, seeing where they are spending their money in this way can help them reprioritize. Anything that makes it easier to budget and then helps you use your budget is a good thing.

Another reason to use automated programs is that they allow you to keep track of all your checking, savings, and investment accounts in one place. But remember—the only way a budget will ever fit perfectly is if you actually use it.

Don't be this girl:

She read Chapters One and Two. She dutifully wrote down all of her actual expenses and made a budget. Then, feeling virtuous for having done so, she promptly went out and spent 120 dollars for a super-snug pair of jeans, forty dollars on drinks with her friends, then later that night ten dollars on a must-see movie plus another two dollars on gummy worms, and, oh yeah, five dollars for a latté the next morning to cure her hangover and reduce her alcohol bloat. She spent 177 dollars that wasn't in her budget and she hardly noticed it disappear from her purse. That can—and will—happen if you don't pay attention.

Do be this girl:

You read Chapters One and Two. You, too, wrote down your expenses and made a budget. By using your budget, you determined before you went out for drinks, in a chic little number you already owned, that you could, and would, only spend twenty dollars on drinks— saving on both calories and cash—and that you would see the movie (ten dollars) but skip the gummy worms. With fewer drinks and a reduced sugar rush, you didn't need a latte the next morning. But since you had budgeted for one, you rewarded yourself—and bumped into the cute guy from the night before. Now you have a date tonight...hello, financial karma!

• • •

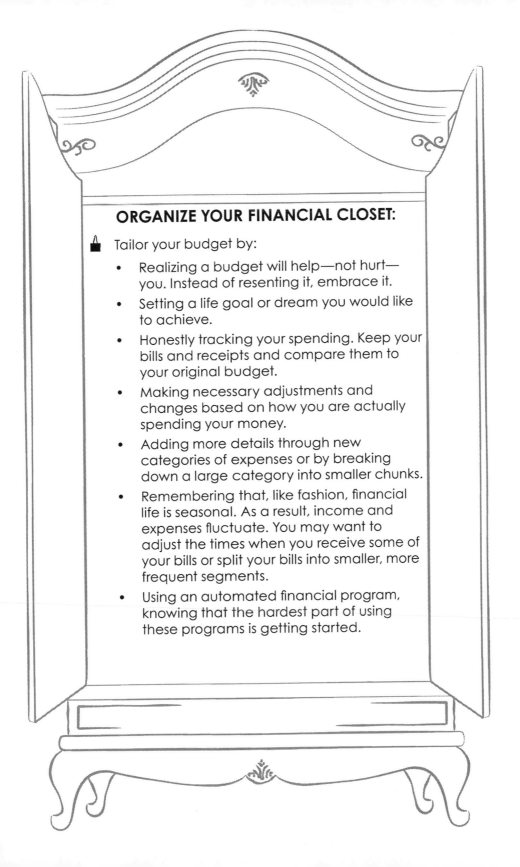

ORGANIZE YOUR FINANCIAL CLOSET:

Tailor your budget by:

- Realizing a budget will help—not hurt—you. Instead of resenting it, embrace it.
- Setting a life goal or dream you would like to achieve.
- Honestly tracking your spending. Keep your bills and receipts and compare them to your original budget.
- Making necessary adjustments and changes based on how you are actually spending your money.
- Adding more details through new categories of expenses or by breaking down a large category into smaller chunks.
- Remembering that, like fashion, financial life is seasonal. As a result, income and expenses fluctuate. You may want to adjust the times when you receive some of your bills or split your bills into smaller, more frequent segments.
- Using an automated financial program, knowing that the hardest part of using these programs is getting started.

Chapter 3: How To Spend

AVOID VISIBLE PANTY LINES (DON'T GIVE AWAY YOUR ASSETS)

You couldn't help it. You were simply walking down the street. You weren't even window-shopping. Then, there they were—the black stilettos you have been looking for practically your *whole* life. The sun was shining and (clearly a sign from the shoe gods) those particular shoes happened to be brilliantly illuminated. Blinded by lust, you ran into the store. I mean, the shoes were glowing—it wasn't your fault. And, besides, black is a neutral, goes with everything, and just last week when you put on your fabulous new skirt, you were thinking once again about how you needed shoes just like these to go with it. Okay, so maybe they were a tad expensive—no, insanely expensive—but you've been working hard. You deserve it. Only as you are signing for them do those annoying thoughts creep in: "This is going to wreak havoc with my budget," and "How many black shoes does a girl really need?" Yes, infinity is a real number, but who has that much closet space, so how is that relevant?

∽ FASHIONISTA FACT: ∽

A poll of 1,057 women by the *Consumer Reports National Research Center* for shopping magazine *ShopSmart* found that U.S. women on average own nineteen pairs of shoes, although they only wear four pairs regularly; 15 percent have over thirty pairs.

Spending is often what we do best. However, knowing how to spend, and when to spend, is critical. What *must* we have? What can we live without? And how do we know which is which? There are not a lot of role models out there for women to follow. What *is* out there is a ton of external pressure to spend, spend, and spend. Consumer products companies spend billions telling us which products we need and why. Retail stores devote a great deal of time, money, and effort to make their store windows stop us in our tracks. Movies, television shows, fashion magazines, and the media's relentless coverage of who wore what all send a message about how much we need to spend and what we need to spend it on in order to look and feel good. Even the federal government overspends and as an all too predictable result, sends us into an economic crisis.

Can we stop the madness? How do we know what to buy and where to spend? Confused priorities can wreck your budget. Four months rent or a Cartier Tank watch? (You might be surprised by how many people—not just women either—decide in favor of their version of the watch.) How do you choose? Start by revisiting your budget. If you can afford the watch—go ahead and buy

> ### ∾ FASHIONISTA FACT: ∾
>
> Among the wristwatches created during the twentieth century, the Tank watch, designed by the master jeweler Louis Cartier, has remained the most long-lived and one of the most coveted. Inspired by the design of the Renault tank, the Tank watch uses the lines and proportions of tanks found on the World War One battlefield.

it. If your budget indicates that you can't, don't despair. You could make it a dream or a goal to save for, or you could pay your rent and shop a notch or two (or three) down, or not at all.

Priorities are different for everyone. How do you know what yours are? Let's start with the basics of needs and wants. What's the difference between the two? A need is something you simply can't do without. It is something you have to have to survive in a reasonably comfortable way. Needs are the basic building blocks of life. Wants are desires. A want is something that, no matter how much you may crave it, you can live just fine without. You *want* the Cartier Tank watch; you *need* to know what time it is. You *want* the black stilettos beckoning from the window; you *need* to have your feet covered, but not with that particular pair of shoes.

You can start to sort your wants versus your needs by looking at the budget categories you created in Chapter One or by using the ones I created. Most of the categories fill needs. Where and how you spend your money within them soon become wants:

Need	Want
Place to live	Your own apartment, a bigger, better place to live, or your own home
Food	Expensive restaurants and fancy drinks
Basic wardrobe (clothes)	Designer labels, to wear to the expensive restaurants
Liability insurance (medical, car, property)	Extra policies and more coverage (life, disability, etc.)
Laundry	Someone else to do it; dry cleaning
Education	Top-notch private school, college or university
Beauty products	Kerastase and Crème de la Mer
Utilities (gas, water, electricity, phone)	Cable, DirectTV, iPhone, iPod
Transportation	Little red convertible; okay make that a Mercedes convertible

By using your budget to review how and where you are spending your money, you will be able to spot potentially problematic trends and fix them before they get out of hand. You might have to make some hard decisions about what it is you need and what you merely want. Only you can sort out which is which, along with what you are willing to give up. And you must stay committed to the rule that only if you have a surplus of funds at the end of every month can you start to purchase things you want, in addition to the things you need.

Once you have thought about your priorities—you would like that little red convertible, but acquiring it would require you to get a roommate versus you hate having a roommate and convertibles have a sun protection factor of zero and therefore cause wrinkles and, God forbid, skin cancer—you can start to think about how, where, or if you want to spend your money. Not spending it is really hard, no question. Nevertheless, it is a really good idea to save some of it even at the cost of not spending.

So back to the stilettos. Yes, they were calling your name from the window, but should you have bought them? Again, if you needed them—and black heels, even black stilettos, are a wardrobe staple—and you knew from your budget that you could afford them, it was okay to buy them. If you wanted them, but knew you couldn't afford them then, no, you shouldn't have bought them, you should have left them in the window to lure someone else into going over her budget. If you didn't need them, and already have multiple pairs of black shoes, but *really* wanted them, then you should also have left them at the store. Sometimes we just have to say no and back away from the object of our desire, no matter how intense that desire may be. Remember, if they are that important to you and you can't afford them right now, you can save the money you need, go back, and get them later. If they no longer have them in your size, chalk it up to shoe karma and move on.

> There is a school of thought that suggests as follows: If you see an expensive item that immediately becomes a want—a burning passion you just can't live without—walk away. If the desire continues unabated for at least five days and you can afford it, go back to the store. If the item is still there, your lust increases on seeing it again, and they have it in your size, congratulations. If it's not there, or they are out of your size, consider yourself saved by karma.

It is your prerogative to be a slave to fashion, and especially expensive designer items, if, but only if, you can afford them. Coco Chanel once said, "Fashion is made to become unfashionable." If you can't afford them—and most of us can't, let's face it—there are always alternatives, notably second label lines, which are cheaper but still high-styled. Smart shopping requires four things: Planning, focus, investing, and finding bargains. Most of the following tips come from *In Style Secrets of Style:*

Plan:

- Figure out what you have and what you need—shop with a list.
- Determine how much money you can spend.
- Shop when you are feeling good about yourself, not when you are bored or upset.
- Shop when stores are the least crowded, so you can get the attention you deserve.
- Dressing well requires strategy, so take your time.

- Know the store's return policy—we all make mistakes and the fashionably and financially responsible thing to do is return the item when that happens.

Focus:

- Shop by yourself—unless you need someone to keep you in check and to tell you to "just back away from the shoes." Friends can distract you and encourage you to buy items you don't need.
- Know what styles work for you and stick to them. Just because something is trendy does not mean it is right for you.
- Buy for the body you have, not the one you want: Spending money on a size four when you are an eight is not smart. Yes, I know you will be a four in no time, but the point is, you're not a four this minute.
- Don't deviate from your plan.

Invest:

- Buy complete outfits, otherwise you will have a closet full of nothing-to-wear. True classics are the exception—black, grey, navy or tan pants, white shirts, classic skirts.

- Buy the best quality you can afford for the classics and scrimp on the trendy stuff.
- Be wary of sale racks. Just because it is on sale does not mean it is a bargain or you need it. You only save money at a sale if it was something you were already looking for.

Bargains:

- Study the deals and steals sections of most fashion magazines.
- Go to your favorite shopping website and check out the sale section (or sign up for their e-mails).
- Bluefly.com: Up to 40 to 70 percent off retail; need I say more?
- Boutique stores: Get on their mailing lists to receive notices of sales.
- Department stores: Look for second lines like Marc by Marc Jacobs and wait until they have a sale.
- Outlet stores
- Sample sales
- Lower scale retailers: Have you been to Target lately?
- Newsletters: www.dailycandy.com can tell you about sales, not to mention fabulous boutiques in your area.

🛍 Thrift shops, known euphemistically as vintage stores; but be forewarned, genuine vintage clothes can cost a bundle.

Last but not least, try, *just try*, to exercise some discipline. Try to avoid winding up with a bunch of fabulous clothes you *wanted* and no money for anything you *need*. **Impulse spending**, or spending thoughtlessly, usually amounts to literally giving away your money. It can be a money management killer because we really do get blinded by shiny new things and don't realize what they are costing us. This example from *Sex and the City* aptly illustrates the point:

Carrie: [In shoe store with Miranda]: Where did all my money go?

Miranda: At four hundred dollars a pop, how many of these do you own? Fifty?

Carrie: Come on…

Miranda: One hundred?

Carrie: Would that be so wrong?

Miranda: Four hundred dollars times one hundred, there's your down payment.

Carrie: That's only four thousand dollars.

Miranda: No, that's *forty* thousand dollars!

Carrie: I spent *forty* thousand dollars on shoes and I have no place to live? I will literally be the old woman who lived in her shoe.

Carrie, with her disregard for her spending habits—tossing off hundreds of dollars for things she doesn't need and will, in all likelihood, never wear—might be incredibly chic but is a very bad financial role model. And marrying a rich man is never a given and rarely the solution.

• • •

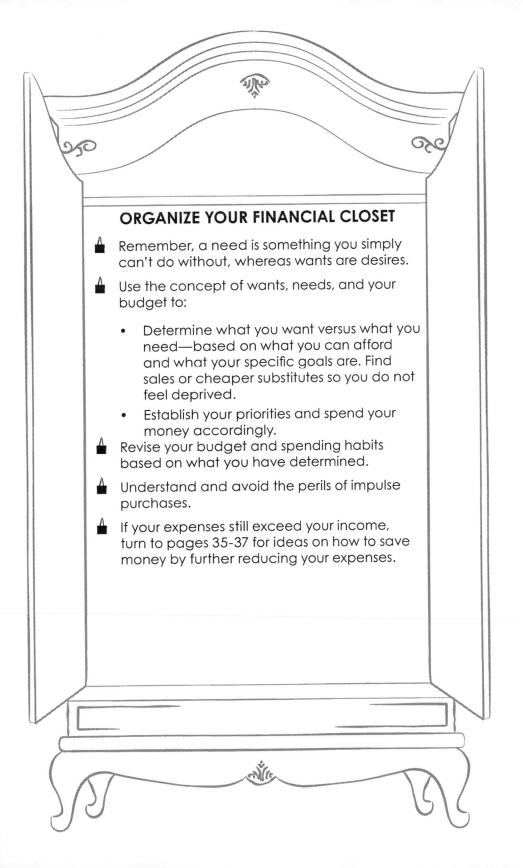

ORGANIZE YOUR FINANCIAL CLOSET

- Remember, a need is something you simply can't do without, whereas wants are desires.

- Use the concept of wants, needs, and your budget to:

    - Determine what you want versus what you need—based on what you can afford and what your specific goals are. Find sales or cheaper substitutes so you do not feel deprived.
    - Establish your priorities and spend your money accordingly.

- Revise your budget and spending habits based on what you have determined.

- Understand and avoid the perils of impulse purchases.

- If your expenses still exceed your income, turn to pages 35-37 for ideas on how to save money by further reducing your expenses.

Chapter 4: How To Save
IF THE BRA FITS (SUPPORT YOUR SHOPPING INDULGENCES)

You are making serious progress. You've now got a budget that's working, you've thought about your wants versus your needs, and you've set some priorities. You know what you earn, what you spend (including where and why), and whether you have anything left over. Extra money equals savings equals shopping! Nothing equals debt equals no shopping! If necessary, please go back and re-work your budget.

Why do you need to have some money left over at the end of the month after you have paid all your bills? Because you want to be in a position where you can start saving. Like a good bra, savings support you if anything goes wrong; for example, your car breaks down, or your rent gets raised, or you lose your job. You don't want to droop every time something unexpected happens. You do want to be able to survive the surprises life throws at you without embarrassment or discomfort.

How much should you have in savings? To start, save up to one month's worth of living expenses. This may take awhile, but it is really crucial. You want to be able to take care of yourself if you hit any bumps. Work your way up to three months and then promise yourself you won't touch that money unless there is an emergency.

So the sooner you start saving, the better. I urge you to start saving now—even if you only have a little bit left over every month. For example, if you are twenty-one and do not have any savings but can start saving one hundred dollars per month (twenty-five dollars per week), and earn five percent interest on your money, by doing nothing more, you will have saved a little over 78,000 dollars by the time you are fifty. If you wait until you are thirty-one to start saving the same one hundred dollars per month, when you are fifty you will have a little less than 38,000 dollars. In this example, waiting ten years to start your savings meant you saved 40,000 dollars less.

The higher the interest, the bigger the difference will become between saving now and saving later. For example, if you start saving the same one hundred dollars per month, when you are twenty-one, but earn a 10 percent interest rate instead of five, you will have approximately 203,000 dollars by the time you are fifty. If you wait another ten years to start saving, when you are fifty you would have 68,000 dollars—135,000 dollars less.

Another reason to save is so that you can afford the big-ticket things you want. It might be an expensive suit, diamond studs, your wedding, a new car, a college education, or a home. Whatever your dream or shopping indulgence, saving money can help you achieve it.

One critical tip: If you have high-interest debt, like credit card debt, pay that off before you start saving.

The minimal interest that savings accounts pay doesn't come close to the interest rates you pay to credit card companies. High interest rates end up costing you a lot of money, money you could be saving instead of giving away to the bank.

Finally, you also want to save for retirement. I realize your golden years seem really far off when you are young. But there is another reason that the sooner you start saving, the faster your money can grow and it's a phenomenon called compounding, which I'll cover in more detail later on.

One great way to start saving is to budget for it. Include a line item in your budget for savings, just as you have for groceries and clothes. To ensure that you add to it regularly, set up an **automatic savings plan**. You can have your bank automatically transfer a designated amount of money from your checking account to your savings account each month. It's a good and pretty painless way to force yourself to save, since almost always out of sight is out of mind. When was the last time you thought about that smashing coat, the one you just had to have but didn't get? My guess is it's been awhile...

It may be that you have been really careful about your spending and still don't have anything left over, but don't despair—if you have a job, march into your boss's office and demand a raise. As long as you have earned it and it has been awhile since you last received one, it is okay to go in and ask for more money. (Obviously, be very prudent about how and when you do this). Many women don't ask for what they are entitled to receive. It is not greedy or bad to ask to insist on being properly compensated. If you don't have a boss and your money comes from your folks or a rich "friend," think about how you might effectively argue for more. To them, you can say, "Look at my budget. I am open to suggestions on additional places to save, but, as you can see, things are already pretty tight. You do want me to be able to have a little fun sometimes, don't you?"

If this approach fails, you can always fall back on the old standby—whining. (Just kidding). Sometimes a second or better paying job is an option. If none of these alternatives feels comfortable, and you cannot find a way to bring in more cash, then I am afraid you will have to go back and figure out how to do more cutting. Goodbye Neiman Marcus, hello J Crew! Goodbye J Crew, hello Gap! Goodbye Gap, hello Target! Goodbye Target, hello vintage!

Again, as with a good bra, savings should fit your needs snugly so you will feel secure; you may find you need a larger income or a smaller budget. Also, as with breasts and bras, the size of your savings account needs will change during the course of your lifetime.

IF YOU NEED EVEN MORE SUPPORT, HAVE A BRA FITTING. ∽

According to Valerie Monroe of *O* magazine, Oprah discovered "eighty-five percent of women wear the wrong-sized bra!" *O* magazine suggests women should: (1) try a smaller band: Most women think comfortable means loose. What they actually need is a firmer band to keep the bra level across the front and back. (2) Try a larger cup: Cup size doesn't remain constant— it increases and decreases proportionally with band size, so if you go to a smaller band, you may need a bigger cup. (3) It pays to upgrade: Buy three top-quality bras rather than a lot of cheapies. You need only one to wear, one to wash, and one in the drawer. (4) The centerpiece shouldn't be more than an inch across.

Saving without bitter regrets

Here are a few ideas on ways to save money that should not feel overly onerous:

- Make a budget and stick to it.
- Start saving now—put away a little bit every month.
- Set up an automatic savings plan (more on this in the next chapter).
- Track your spending.
- Pay all your bills in full every month and avoid high-interest debts.
- Avoid most debt. Student loans and mortgages can be "good" debt, although paying them off should be a priority.
- Stop smoking! Not only will you save money now—on the cigarettes, on dry cleaners to get out that nasty smell, and on teeth whiten-

ing—but also in the future, when you don't need lip fillers from the dermatologist or, God forbid, an oncologist.

- Eat in more often.
- Pay your savings account one dollar for every workout, two dollars if it was a really hard one. If you manage five hard workouts per week, you will be healthier, thinner, and have ten more dollars in your savings account.
- Buy a used car or take public transportation. Even better, walk or bike or run. Obviously this is not always possible. But think of the calories you will burn and money you will save on a gym membership.
- Patience can be a virtue—today's "It bag" will be adorning tomorrow's sale rack.
- Discounts can be your best friend or your worst enemy—you only save money if it's something you really need.
- Never buy warranties—they're a bad bet.
- Go green. Look for ways to save on utilities and in other areas. For example, you could change your light bulbs to fluorescent or lower your heat.
- Make sure you have the right cell phone plan for your needs or check out Voice Over IP (VOIP) if you make a lot of long distance calls.

- Don't pay banking fees—use ATMs that are free for your bank.
- Don't rent DVDs or games—get them free from the library or join Netflix for no late fees. (But don't join Netflix at even the cheapest level and then hold onto one DVD for three months.)
- Cut down on that snack habit (two four-dollar trips to the vending machine equals eight dollars per day. Eight dollars a day times 365 days equals 2,920 dollars. You only go once? That's still 1,460 dollars per year. And don't even talk to me about the candy bars.)

• • •

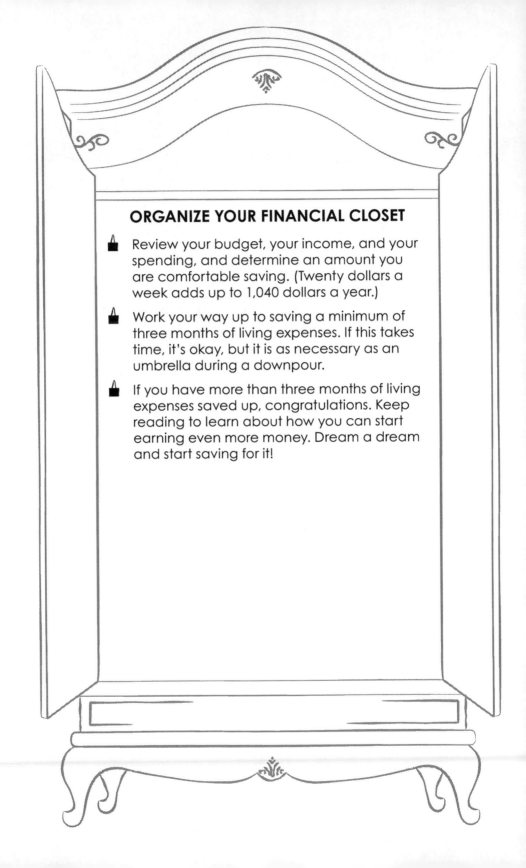

ORGANIZE YOUR FINANCIAL CLOSET

- Review your budget, your income, and your spending, and determine an amount you are comfortable saving. (Twenty dollars a week adds up to 1,040 dollars a year.)

- Work your way up to saving a minimum of three months of living expenses. If this takes time, it's okay, but it is as necessary as an umbrella during a downpour.

- If you have more than three months of living expenses saved up, congratulations. Keep reading to learn about how you can start earning even more money. Dream a dream and start saving for it!

Chapter 5: Bank Accounts
IT'S IN THE BAG (WHERE TO KEEP YOUR MONEY)

Shoulder bags, clutches, and totes...oh my! By pulling together an outfit and giving you a place to carry your ever-expanding pile of belongings, the right bag makes your life easier and, yes, better, but it is not the only place you should keep your money. In fact, even the best-looking bag is a lousy place to stash it. Here's why:

- Your purse can get stolen.
- Your purse is not insured.
- Your purse doesn't keep track of where or how you spend your money.
- Your purse does not pay interest. When you open a savings account at a bank, the bank pays you money for leaving your money with them. This is called interest. Interest on even a small bank balance will buy you a cupcake in a month. Has your purse ever bought you a cupcake? Different kinds of accounts pay different interest rates and you earn more or less money depending on what kind of account it is.
- Your purse does not offer any of the benefits bank accounts offer. One example is overdraft protection, which means a bank will cover you for a short time if you write a check but do not have the funds in your account to pay for it.

🛍 The best places to keep your money are in a checking and savings account in a bank or in other financial institutions, such as a savings and loans or a credit union. This may seem basic and obvious. But just as the right purse can pull an outfit together, so can keeping your money in the right place pull your financial life together.

∽ **FASHIONISTA FACT:** ∽

Purses have been used by men and women for an incredibly long time. Originally they were used to carry seeds and in religious ceremonious—living up to their status as *holy*. By the 1400s, both men and women were carrying purses, and, as times prospered, purses were ornamented with gold or elaborate embroidery. A century later, the drawstring bag was a status possession and has remained one ever since.

Let's start with **checking accounts**. A checking account is as basic and as necessary as a black shoulder bag. Checking accounts are provided by financial institutions so you have a place where you can deposit and withdraw your money on a frequent basis. Checking accounts let you write checks and, more often than not, checking accounts also offer debit cards or Automatic Teller Machine (ATM) cards as another way of letting you access your account and take out cash. A debit card takes money directly from your checking (or savings) account. It is just like paying with cash. Checking accounts pay a minimal amount of interest on your account.

HOW TO CHOOSE A CHECKING ACCOUNT

Every girl needs a checking account. After budgeting, it is step two of a sound financial plan. To open one, you *could* pick the first bank you see, but why would you? Just as you *could* pick the first great-looking black shoulder bag you see, but wouldn't. Instead, it's best when scouting for both bags and banks to spend some time looking, to find the one that best suits your particular needs.

To begin, visit banks and credit unions in your area. What, no time to do this? Let your fingers do the typing and search online. What are you looking for? At minimum, the right checking account will have:

- Low fees
- Free online banking
- Overdraft protection—in case you bounce a check or, worse, have an emergency

Beyond these basic requirements, questions to ask as you are shopping—and, yes, it is shopping; just because it doesn't come home in a bag with you doesn't mean it's not shopping—include:

1. What kind of services does the bank offer?
2. What are their fees? There are all kinds of fees: Fees for bounced checks, fees for writing more checks than allowed, teller fees, calling fees, and fees for paper copies of your statements. Some also have monthly service fees.

3. Does the account pay interest? How often and how much?

4. Do they offer debit cards?

5. Do they offer online banking? Do they charge for it?

6. Do they offer **overdraft protection**? Do they charge for it? If you have overdraft protection, rather than returning the bounced check to the person you wrote it to, the bank covers your payment until you add another deposit and then they take back the money they lent you and often add in a fee. Do not bounce checks—it is irresponsible and definitely not chic!

7. Do they have credit cards? Sometimes banks offer better deals on accounts if you have more than one account with them. However, be sure to choose the best credit card for you—which may not be the card the bank offers. (For more on how to choose a credit card see page 68.)

8. Is there a minimum balance you have to maintain?

9. Can you get an ATM card with the account?

10. Can you electronically download from your account into a financial software program? There are lots of computer programs to help you manage your money, and many banks allow you to automatically download your information so you don't need to type it in.

11. Is the bank FDIC-insured?

How do you know which answers are the right ones for you? By understanding your own habits and needs. Who knows you better than you? How many checks do you write each month? Do you bounce checks often enough that you might need overdraft protection? (If so, stop it right now!) Is the amount of money you will be able to keep in the account enough to meet their minimum? Once you have a clear idea of your habits, you can find an account to match your needs. There are websites that compare features and rates of different checking accounts side by side. Bankrate.com is one example. Now, if only ferreting out shoulder bags were so easy.

A few other checking account thoughts: When you order checks, pay the extra money the bank charges for security mailing. You don't want your checks to get stolen out of your mailbox. Also, never put your driver's license, social security number, or telephone number on your checks. No need to disseminate valuable information to people you don't know. In fact, it's a good idea to just use your first initial instead of your whole first name on your checks. That way, if someone steals your checks they won't know your entire name. This is a good tip for your mailbox, too, and even your listing in the phone book. Finally, if you are not good at writing down and keeping track of the checks you have written in the **checkbook register,** get checks in duplicate with carbon paper under each check so you automatically have a record of every check you write.

Next let's talk about **savings accounts.** In handbag terms, they're like a clutch that goes from day to evening; in other words, quite versatile. Savings accounts are provided by the same kinds of financial institutions that provide checking accounts, but they don't usually have a check-writing feature. To access money that you have in a savings account, you will probably need to visit the bank or use an ATM. Their advantage is that they let you set aside a portion of your money and earn more in interest on it than if you left all of your money in a checking account.

Although there are lots of clutches to choose from (day, evening, cocktail, mini, satin, leather, jeweled, feathered, embroidered), there are only three basic kinds of savings accounts:

- Basic savings account
- Money market account
- Certificates of deposit (CD)

A basic savings account is sometimes called a **passbook savings account**. Usually you can keep any amount of money you want in a basic savings account, with no minimum balance required. They pay interest rates that are higher than checking accounts, but lower than the rates paid by the other two kinds of savings accounts. You can withdraw your money whenever you want.

A **money market** savings account often requires you to keep a higher minimum balance—sometimes as high as 2,500 dollars—in your account than in a regular savings account and, in exchange, pays you higher interest. But there can be a downside: A money market sometimes prevents you from withdrawing any of your money for a fixed period of time and may limit the number of withdrawals you can make—often three to six—in a month.

But don't sweat it. Limiting withdrawals is a good thing when it comes to savings. If your budget is well constructed and you are staying within it, then you should not have to withdraw money from your savings account unless you have an emergency or reach a goal.

In addition to following the advice from How to Choose a Checking Account, when you are shopping for a savings account, you might want to find out how the interest rate is paid—fixed or variable and what limits there are on your ability to withdraw your money. Interest can be **fixed,** meaning the bank pays you the same amount of interest each time, based on a pre-agreed upon amount, or **variable,** meaning the bank pays you a different amount of interest each time, based on how interest rates, which go up and down depending on a variety of factors, are performing. Savings accounts and money markets typically pay variable rates. This can be good or bad for you, obviously depending on whether rates are going up, in which case you will earn more interest, or down, in which case you will earn less.

Just as you shop for the best checking account, so you should shop for the best savings account. Sometimes banks charge fees for accounts. Find one that doesn't. Often banks will offer you a good deal if you open both accounts at the same place—kind of like a buy one, get one free sale.

A **certificate of deposit** (CD for short—and known as such long before the kind that plays music was invented) is another type of savings account. A CD is rather like a tote bag—it holds quadruple the amount a normal bag can accommodate, but is it the right size for you?

A CD differs from both a savings account and a money market account in that your money goes into a CD for a specific, fixed period of time (often three months, six months, or one to five years), and, in return, the bank will usually pay you a fixed interest rate. But during the period of time that you've signed up for you really don't have access to it.

A savings account, like a checking account, can be kept open forever. You can deposit and, except for some savings account restrictions, withdraw your money almost as often as you need. But with CDs, the bank is relying on you to keep your money in place, so they charge you a penalty for early withdrawal. The penalties are rarely waived except in extreme circumstances. Desperately needed resort wear for that unexpected trip to St. Barts would not qualify.

Once the period you selected ends, you get back all of your money plus the interest it earned for you. Then you can decide if you want to re-invest your money in another CD, selecting perhaps a different period, or save it in a savings account or money market, or spend it. Why would you choose the restrictions of a CD over a savings account? Not only because of the higher rate of interest, but also because of the fact that you can't take your money out early without incurring penalties, which will lessen the temptation to do so. Thus, under the right set of circumstances, CDs can offer certain advantages. But, like that over-sized tote, they can also be packed with things you don't want or need.

∾ FOUR TIPS FOR CD GLORY ∾

1. Be sure the bank you buy the CD from is FDIC-insured.
2. Don't put money in a CD that you think you may need before the CD is scheduled to mature, to avoid paying a penalty for early withdrawal.
3. If your CD is almost mature and you are going to need to have the money back, let the bank know in advance. If you don't, the bank may "roll over" the CD, meaning they will automatically re-invest your money in a new CD for the same maturing period and, once again, you won't be able to touch your money again for the same amount of time.
4. Don't take interest early. Some banks offer to pay you the interest via a check. Don't utilize this option. Leave the interest in the CD to compound with the rest of your money.

To sum up: The differences between passbook savings, money market, and CD accounts are access and interest rates. The more difficult it is to access your money and the longer the time period before you can withdraw it, the higher the interest rate you will receive.

Good money management requires you have a checking account, for day-to-day life, and some sort of savings account for emergencies and to help build your future.

Now, let's discuss **online banking**. I know you already know all about online shopping. Online banking is no different; your bank offers you access to your account online. You can check your balance, pay bills (saving you money on checks and stamps), and even download your deposits and withdrawals electronically into an automated financial program, making it easy for you to see and track your actual spending against your budget. So now you have no excuses.

One final note: Both savings and checking accounts are federally insured through the **Federal Deposit Insurance Corporation** or **FDIC**. FDIC insurance protects you from losses if your bank goes bankrupt. Although banks are usually very safe places to keep your money, they do loan your money out and invest it in a variety of ways. The people in charge of banks are not always as careful with your money as you are. It's rare, but as we saw in 2008, banks *can* go out of business so it's important to be protected. The federal government guarantees up to 250,000 dollars per depositor (that's you) and up to 250,000 dollars for retirement accounts (401Ks and IRAs). Credit unions are insured up to the same level through the **National Credit Union Administration** or **NCUA**. So your money really is safer in a financial institution than in a purse, no matter how closely held. Baby, you got a brand new bag!

∾ FASHIONISTA FACT: ∾

Investment bags, bags that will last you a lifetime and that will truly never go out of style but which will require you to forgo your rent include: The Chanel 2.55, Louis Vuitton Speedy, Gucci's Jackie O, and the Hermes Birkin bag.

• • •

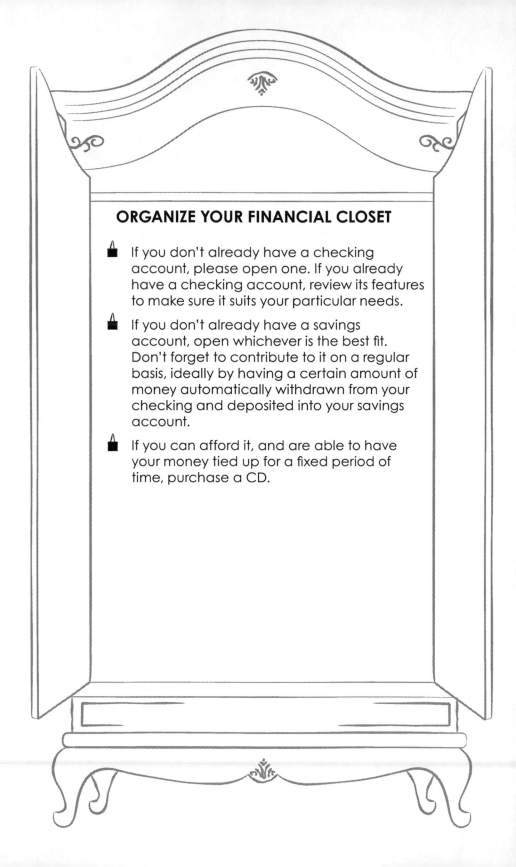

ORGANIZE YOUR FINANCIAL CLOSET

- If you don't already have a checking account, please open one. If you already have a checking account, review its features to make sure it suits your particular needs.

- If you don't already have a savings account, open whichever is the best fit. Don't forget to contribute to it on a regular basis, ideally by having a certain amount of money automatically withdrawn from your checking and deposited into your savings account.

- If you can afford it, and are able to have your money tied up for a fixed period of time, purchase a CD.

How to reconcile your checking account

You should reconcile your checking account every month. The bank statement includes instructions and a worksheet for balancing your checking account with the bank statement. Feel free to follow their instructions or mine—there is no one, single right way to balance your account. What's important is you do it! Here's how:

Step one:

In your checkbook, record every single check you write, every single check you deposit, and every single ATM withdrawal you make. If you are not so good about recording what checks you write when you write them, then you should order checks with duplicate copies. The checkbook will come with carbon copies under each check that trace every check you write. You won't have to do a thing. Well, that's not quite true. You will still have to write down your deposits and ATM withdrawals.

Step two:

Keep all of the statements the bank sends you. Each month, compare the entries you made in your checkbook with those in your bank statement. Take a pen and mark off in your checkbook every transaction you see on your statement.

If you see entries on your statement that are not in your checkbook because you forgot to write them down, add them in now. For example, if the bank paid you interest, you will want to add it to your checkbook as a deposit; or if you forgot to write down a check now is the time to include it as a withdrawal. The goal is to find any discrepancies between the statement and the checkbook.

Step three:

On your bank statement, find the final balance, also called the ending balance. It is the total of all of the cash that has been added and taken out of your account.

Step four:

Go back to your checkbook. Are there any deposits that are not checked off? If so, this means you made a deposit that was added to your account after the cutoff date for your bank statement. Add those deposits to the final balance on your bank statement.

Step five:

Look at your checkbook one more time. Are there any checks, ATM fees, or other withdrawals that are not checked off? This means you wrote a check or made a withdrawal after the cutoff date for that bank statement. Subtract those from the final balance on your bank statement.

Your checkbook and your final statement should now match. If they don't, go back and try to figure out why. Make sure you didn't leave anything out. Did you

write down all the checks?
ATM fees? Service charges?
Automatic deposits? Interest? Did you mark every-
thing off? Did you check
your math? If you answered
yes to all of these questions
and if the discrepancy is a

> If your checkbook and bank state-
> ment don't match by a little bit—
> like a few cents—just add or sub-
> tract the difference to your check-
> book. If you are off by more than a
> few cents, though, go back and see
> if you can figure out why.

small one, then let it go. Sometimes these things happen, like socks mysteriously losing their mates in the laundry. Just make sure there are no unfamiliar charges on
your bank statement. If there are, call the bank immediately so you can determine if you have a theft problem.
To fix the fact that you do not match, add or subtract
to your checkbook the amount you are out of balance
so your checkbook register and your bank statement
match.

You do not actually have to do all of this by hand,
although it's good to do so at least once so you understand how it works. But there are plenty of computer programs and websites to help you reconcile these figures,
and some of them are even free. Just Google "free excel
checking account reconciliation" and pick out a spread-
sheet. They are already set up and automated, so all
you have to do is find one that feels comfortable to you.
You still have to type in your specific information—what
checks you wrote and what deposits you made, or at
least the totals—but the math will all be automated. Also,

any good financial program (for example Quicken, Microsoft Money, or mint.com), which I strongly encourage you to buy and use, will have an automated balance feature. These programs are better than the free programs because they integrate your financial life in one place. In addition to your checkbook, they track your savings and investments accounts as well as the value of your assets (big-ticket items you own) and your debts (student loans, credit cards, and mortgages). By tracking all of your financial information, these programs can help you see your financial situations and manage your finances as an integrated whole. These programs also allow you to automatically download your transactions so you won't have to type them in. Trust me, in the long term, having and using a financial program is one of the best investments you can make for, and in, yourself.

• • •

Chapter 6: Debit Cards
JEANS & TEES (WHAT YOU JUST CAN'T LIVE WITHOUT)

A great-fitting pair of jeans is likely to be the most favored thing in your closet. And a good tee is also a wardrobe staple. Whether under a suit, with those much loved jeans, or at the gym, the right tee is always there for you. Sharon Stone even wore one once to the Oscars. Similarly, a debit card should be the most favored thing in your wallet *and* a staple of your financial wardrobe.

> "I wish I had invented blue jeans. They have expression, modesty, sex appeal, and simplicity—all I hope for in my clothes." Yves Saint Laurent

Although it looks and acts like a credit card, a **debit card** is, essentially, an extension of your checking or savings account. It takes money directly from either account, depending on which account you instruct the bank to use. Unlike credit cards, for which you receive a bill for purchases made over a one-month period, debit cards take (or debit) the money from your account immediately. It is just like paying with cash, but better, because you have a record of what you bought in addition to a sales slip. Any purchase made with your debit card is automatically itemized on your bank statement, which helps you track your money. You'll know what you have and how you spent it—the Holy Grail of budgeting!

A debit card offers you some of the benefits a credit card does. For example, you can pay for things over the Internet or on the phone, you can use it at places that accept credit cards, and you can use it at places that do not accept checks. And, in addition, there are no fees or interest charges to use debit cards. In fact, if you have a debit card that charges you fees to use it, cancel it and get a new one that doesn't.

However—and this is key—as with cash and credit cards, debit cards can be stolen. But unlike with cash or credit cards, with debit cards the thief could gain access to your entire checking or savings account. Debit cards from major card issuers such as Visa or MasterCard carry the same fraud protections as credit cards, with zero liability, but some others don't. Either way, you'll want to report a stolen card as soon as possible. If you report the loss within two days, you will be responsible for only fifty dollars of charges. However, if you don't report the loss within sixty days, you could owe up to five hundred dollars for any transactions made by the thief. Remember how I urged you to check your accounts regularly in Chapter Five? That's one of the reasons.

There are other disadvantages to debit cards, one being you can only spend what's in your account. (Of course, I happen to think that is a good thing.) Each time you use the card, you have to remember if you have written any checks that are outstanding. If, for example, you forgot you had recently written a check from that account and mistakenly assumed your account balance was still what your account balance said, when the check you'd previously written reached the bank, it would bounce because it would be drawing on money no longer there. This is where having a checking account with overdraft protection can come in handy. Another disadvantage to a debit card is that if you have no credit, or lousy credit, and are trying to rebuild your credit, using a debit card will not help you.

However, the ability of debit cards to keep you out of trouble by preventing high credit card debt, forcibly controlling your spending by not letting you take out more than you have in your account and tracking your spending, definitely makes them worth considering.

You should also be aware of **prepaid cards,** debit cards that have had a specific amount of money put on them either by you or someone else. Instead of having the card linked to a bank account, you, or whoever might be buying you the card, can tell the bank how much money to put on it and that will be all you get—unless you or they add more to the card when it runs out.

On the plus side, prepaid cards are safer to use than cash and more flexible than single-store gift cards. You can also use them online for purchases and to pay bills.

However, the negatives outweigh the positives. Prepaid cards frequently charge a fee for almost every single thing you do with them. Fair to say, this is not true for every card. If you shop around you might be able to find a prepaid card that meets your needs. You must read the fine print, though. Want to get a card—there is an issuance fee. Want to sign up—there is an enrollment fee. Want to find out how much is left on the card—teller fee. Lose your card and need a new one—replacement fee. Use the card—transaction fee. Don't use the card—inactivity fee. Want to put more money on the card—reload fee. All these fees add up quickly, leaving you less money to spend. In addition, because prepaid cards are not linked to a bank account, like debit cards, they do not help you build your credit. However, there a few new cards out that will report your prepaid card transactions to the credit agencies. In theory, this may help you build a positive profile, but it is still unclear. All in all, you are much better off with a regular debit card.

If someone insists on giving you a prepaid card, be sure they or you have carefully read its "Terms and Conditions." This is the section in a purchase agreement where all those pesky fees show up. Or you can perhaps suggest that, "instead of getting me a prepaid card, how about we use all those fees we saved by not getting the card to buy me an [insert item here]." Let's see—new clothes or fees, new clothes or fees—I'd go with new clothes!

IDENTITY THEFT

It's hardly news that a person can create different identities by changing clothes, make-up, and hair—look at Madonna's entire career. You can channel Nicole Ritchie's bohemian hippie-chick at a moment's notice. Gwen Stefani's glam-punk look is a piece of cake. Kate Moss's effortless chic, no problem. Unfortunately, it's also just about that easy for someone to steal *your* identity. **Identity theft** happens when someone else uses your personal information (name, social security number, or credit card) without your permission—stealing your identity and your money to make purchases illegally in your name.

How do the bad guys get your information? Sometimes it's as simple as "dumpster diving," taking information from papers you might have thrown away—such as a credit card bill or bank statement with your name, address, and account number. Sometimes they "phish" for it, which is to say they create fake websites that pretend to be your bank or credit card company and ask you for information such as your password. Sometimes when you are at a store, they skim the information off your debit or credit card by means of a special storage device installed on a cash register. They can also steal your wallet or purse the old-fashioned way, all in an effort to get your financial information.

So what's a girl to do to prevent this from happening?

- Shred or tear up your personal information before throwing it away. Buy a cheap shredder and use it on all of your personal information—it can come in handy on old love letters and on pictures of your ex-boyfriend, too.

- Check your accounts regularly and look for charges or withdrawals that aren't yours.

- Protect your information with an unusual password or one that uses a combination of letter and numbers. Don't use easy-to-find information such as your birthday, home address, or telephone number.

- Be sure you know you are on the correct website. For example, type in the web address of your bank each time you check your online account; never hit "reply" or click a link from an e-mail from a bank, credit card company, or any other e-mail asking for account or password information.

- Don't provide personal information to folks who call on the phone. For example, if your bank is calling, they already have the information; if you are unsure, get the number and call them back.

- Check out the federal government's website www.ftc.gov/bcp/edu/microsites/idtheft/consumers/deter-detect-defend for more tips.

What do you do if the worst has happened and someone does steal your identify?

- File a police report.
- Notify the three credit agencies (see Chapter 11).
- Notify your bank, debit card, credit card, and investment companies to dispute any charges that are not yours. It will take a lot of time, energy, and effort, but you can clear your name and get your identity back. By the way, most credit cards offer you protection by providing a loss limit, but only if you call them promptly to report a problem.

And if you find yourself channeling Nicole, Gwen, and Kate on a regular basis, consider creating your own personal signature style instead. Unless you are truly a rara avis you will probably save money on clothes and accessories and may end up obtaining Fashionista status. Both your identity and your style should be all your own!

• • •

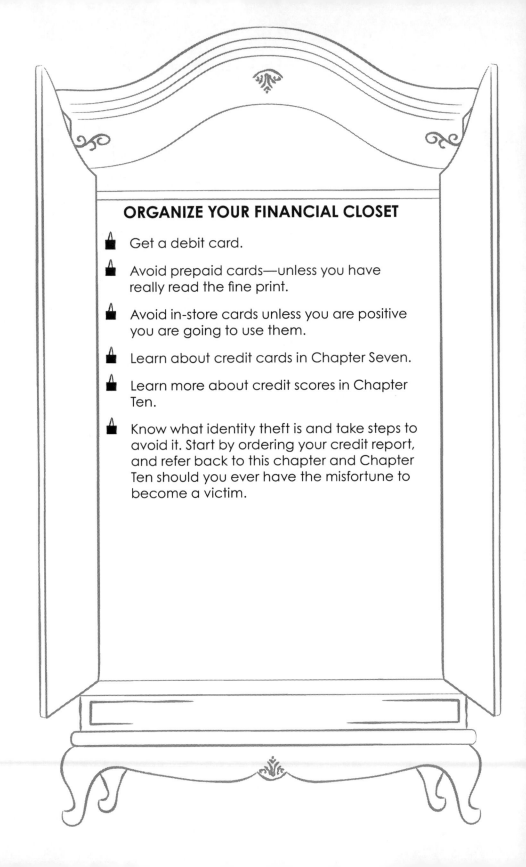

ORGANIZE YOUR FINANCIAL CLOSET

- Get a debit card.

- Avoid prepaid cards—unless you have really read the fine print.

- Avoid in-store cards unless you are positive you are going to use them.

- Learn about credit cards in Chapter Seven.

- Learn more about credit scores in Chapter Ten.

- Know what identity theft is and take steps to avoid it. Start by ordering your credit report, and refer back to this chapter and Chapter Ten should you ever have the misfortune to become a victim.

Chapter 7: Credit Cards
LITTLE BLACK DRESS (ONLY ON SPECIAL OCCASSIONS)

Coveted, overworked, and relied on. The little black dress (LBD). It's every girl's best friend. The right one can command a room and change the course of an evening, if not your whole life. The LBD is very powerful. So is a **credit card**. A credit card is a small, but very potent, piece of plastic. It allows you to buy something now, today, this minute, when you want it, on credit, so you can have it for free—until the bill comes. It, too, can change your whole life—but not always for the better.

Why not for the better? When you charge something on a credit card, you are borrowing money from the credit card company. Since there really is no such thing as a free lunch or dinner... often someone wants *something* for it, unless you pay the bill in full each month, in return for letting you borrow from them, the card companies will charge you a fee. These charges are called

> ∾ **FASHIONISTA FACT:** ∾
> Prior to the 1920s, black dresses were reserved for periods of mourning. It was otherwise considered indecent to wear them. In 1926, *Vogue* published a picture of a short, simple black dress designed by Coco Chanel. It was calf-length, straight, and decorated with a few diagonal lines. It was simple and accessible for women of all social classes and ages. *Vogue* opined that the black dress would become "a sort of uniform for all women of taste" and thus the little black dress was born.

interest and the amount of interest is called the **Annual Percentage Rate** (or **APR**). When you are unable to pay your bill in full every month, the charges for borrowing money from the credit card company add up *very* quickly. APRs are tricky and there are always more than one.

There are APRs for **purchases, cash advances,** *and* **balance transfers.** There are **tiered** *APRs, which means* different rates applied to different levels of the outstanding balance. For example, a credit card company may charge X percent on balances of one hundred to five hundred dollars and Y percent on balances above five hundred dollars. There is a **penalty** APR, which you are charged if you are late in paying the APR or skip a payment. Often there are **introductory** APRs. Credit card companies sometimes offer low rates to get your business to lure you into borrowing money from them, and then increase the rate after a certain amount of time. There is even a **delayed** APR. This means that a rate different from the rate you are paying today will apply in the future. For example, a card may advertise that there is "no interest until next year," which means you pay zero percent until January 1, but then pay but some other, much higher, rate thereafter.

You need to look at APRs very carefully. To make matters even more complicated, while APRs are quoted on an annual basis (meaning yearly), many credit cards quote fees on a daily, weekly, or monthly basis. In Chapter Eight you will learn how the differences in APR timing affect the total you owe the credit card company. All you need to know now is that APR's are dangerous.

When you get your credit card bill, you have a few options: Pay the bill in full, pay some portion of the bill, pay the minimum amount due, or pay nothing and be late. With the exception of paying the bill in full, you will be charged interest. If you don't pay the bill at all, you will be charged a late fee. Interest and late fee charges add up quickly. But if you pay your credit card bill in full every month, none of these charges apply. So not paying your credit card bill in full every month is one of the worst things you can do for your finances. Except in emergencies, switch to using a debit card and pay off as much of your bill as you can. If you are unable to pay your bill in full when you receive it, pay off as much of it as you possibly can. Do not use the card again until you have completely paid your bill and have a zero balance. The lower your outstanding balance (what you still owe the credit card company), the less interest you will owe. Remember, interest is calculated on the amount outstanding. If you pay only the minimum required, you will be paying the credit card company a lot of interest over time. Wouldn't you rather keep your money for yourself? Of course you would.

On the plus side, credit cards help you establish and build up your credit. They do this by providing you with credit and a **credit limit** that is the total amount they have decided to allow you to borrow on the card.

A lot of people move their credit card balances from a credit card with high interest charges to a credit card with lower interest charges. And then, when the interest charges increase, they do it again. If you have a high balance on one or two or three high interest cards and cannot pay them off, or can only make the minimum payments, then there is definitely a benefit to consolidating your balances and moving them to a lower interest card. That way, you can start to pay more than just the minimal balance and reduce your debt. If you do this, be sure to look for a credit card with a consistently lower interest rate—not one with a low teaser rate that will increase again in six months. Also, if you find yourself in this situation, do not use your credit cards until you have paid down what you owe.

Why is this important? How you have handled credit is the main criterion lenders use to decide whether you are trustworthy enough to loan money to. If you have good credit because you have always paid back what you borrowed, you will be permitted to borrow more and pay lower interest rates than if you have bad credit. Bad credit means your track record shows you do not always pay back what you borrow in a timely fashion or at all and are, therefore, not a good credit risk.

If you have been with your credit card company for a while and are in good standing with them—meaning you don't owe them money or you are current on what you owe—you can request to have your credit limit raised. If your credit is good, credit card companies are often willing to work hard to keep you using their card. Sometimes they will even offer to lower your interest rates or waive the annual fee, if there is one.

There are no rules about how many credit cards you should have. However, you really do not need more than two. You should use one for your day-to-day needs and keep one for emergencies. Any more serve as temptation, and shopping is already tempting enough. But if you currently have a lot of credit cards, don't cancel them unless they have high annual fees. Canceling accounts that are in good standing hurts your credit score.

Here is the best way to think about credit cards: You know that little black dress tucked away in your closet; the one that cost a fortune and you only wear once in a while but it's fierce? That should be you and your relationship with your credit card, only on special occasions. There is no doubt that credit cards can come in handy. So can expensive little black dresses. Use both sparingly.

∾ FASHIONISTA FACT: ∾

The most famous example of credit cards, dresses, and special occasions combined was the dress Australian Lizzy Gardiner wore in 1994 when she won an Oscar for Best Costume Design for *The Adventures of Priscilla Queen of the Desert*. The dress was made entirely of American Express Gold Cards, provided in her name, but one number short to invalidate them. The dress was later auctioned for 12,650 dollars, with the proceeds going to the American Foundation for AIDS Research.

How to choose a credit card

You're out shopping. You reach into your purse and whip out:

- Your debit card because you are sticking to your budget and are using cash.
- Your credit card, because you are sticking to your budget but those miles you're racking up will eventually take you to Mexico!

If you chose your credit card, I assume you are planning to pay your bill in full. If you are not, stop the sale and back quickly out of the store.

There are so many credit cards to choose from that it's hard to know which the right ones for you are. Money back? Miles? Perks? A percentage to a worthy cause? If you are shopping for a credit card, especially if it's for the first time, you need to wade through the sexy features. Credit card companies offer all kinds of seductive features to get you to choose their card. Tall, dark, and handsome—or blond, built surfer? The best card for you is the one most closely matching your needs and how you'll use it. Here are questions to ask yourself:

- Are you planning to pay your bill in full every month, as you know you should? If you are, and you want to spend as little as possible on obtaining a credit card, then you want to focus on finding a credit card with no annual fee.

That way, it will not cost you anything at all to have a credit card. Many credit cards with no annual fees do offer perks, but the perks will probably be less alluring than those offered by credit cards that charge you to have them.

How important are the perks? If you plan to pay your bill in full every month and believe that sexy perks, such as earning airline miles, are worth the usual annual fee, then you will want to focus on the best combination of features for you. Perks operate by giving you points for every dollar you spend, usually a very small fraction of a dollar. Perks include airline miles, concierge services, discounts, hotel and car rentals, money back on purchases, and discounts at your favorite store. Choose the perk that excites you the most.

What happens if you don't pay the bill in full? If you know that chances are that occasionally you won't be able to do so and therefore will need to carry a balance, you should focus on credit cards with low interest rates. This is where many of those APRs we discussed before come into play. You need to read the fine print of any credit card you are considering to find the lesser of the evils for your particular circumstances.

Do you use your credit card for cash advances? If you think you might borrow money from your credit card by using a cash advance, you'll want to look for a card that carries lower interest rates *and* lower fees on cash advances. Some cards charge a higher interest rate for cash advances than for purchases. Be aware that borrowing cash on a credit card is one of the most expensive ways to borrow money because of the high interest rates most credit card companies charge.

Once you choose the credit card that is right for you, don't be swayed by other sexier offers. Stick with the one you selected. Your perks accumulate faster if you use only one card, there is only one bill to pay, and it is easier to track and control your spending.

One other tip about credit card offers that arrive in the mail: Don't just throw them away, rip them up or shred them first. You wouldn't want someone to find the application, fill it out, and fly off to South America using your credit unbeknownst to you, would you?

HOW TO BECOME YOUR CREDIT CARD'S BEST FRIEND FOREVER (BFF)

Credit cards—love them or hate them? Love them when we get what we want, when we want it ... which is now! Hate them when we get the bill.

How to smooth out your relationship? Borrowing from credit card companies is way different from borrowing from your friends. For example, let's say you are out with some friends and you order a cappuccino. You reach into your wallet and realize you forgot to bring it, no cash or credit cards. So you borrow five dollars from your friend and agree to pay her back as soon as possible, or that you will buy next time. The fact that you had to borrow five dollars from your friend did not cost you anything more than what you would have spent anyway.

Now let's say you don't see her for a whole month. You were busy; she has this new boyfriend whom you can't stand, blah, blah, blah. They break up, she calls you, and out you go for another cappuccino. You buy her the cappuccino you owe her, listen to how awful the boyfriend was, and now you are even. What are friends for?

Had you borrowed the same five dollars from the credit card company and not been able to pay the bill back right away, the credit card company would have charged you interest plus a late fee. They would also have charged you a fee for every single day you didn't pay the bill. Wait, it gets worse. The fee they charge you every single day is added to the fee they charged you yesterday so every day you don't pay them they wind up charging you more.

It would be as if your friend said: "I let you borrow a cappuccino from me for five dollars. But I am going to charge you an interest fee of five cents for every day we don't have a cappuccino together—never mind that I didn't see you because of the boyfriend I've since dumped. So you will owe me $5.05 if I see you on Monday, $5.10 if I see you Tuesday, and $5.15 if I don't get to see you until Wednesday."

This concept is called compounding. Compounding is when you are charged a fee on the original amount you borrowed (the principal) plus a fee for any money you have not paid back. Credit card companies calculate this charge every day, charging fees on your fees. So what you owe them tomorrow will be more than what you owe them today.

The longer you wait to pay, the bigger the amount you owe becomes. Think that's bad? What if your friend also charged you a late fee of one dollar every day? Week? Month? If you saw her on Wednesday, you would owe her $6.15. If you didn't see your friend for a whole month, she would charge you $7.50—practically two cappuccinos.

So the only way to be your credit card's BFF is to use it only when you know you have enough money to pay the bill in full when it arrives. Otherwise you are signing up for a tortured, miserable, hateful relationship.

• • •

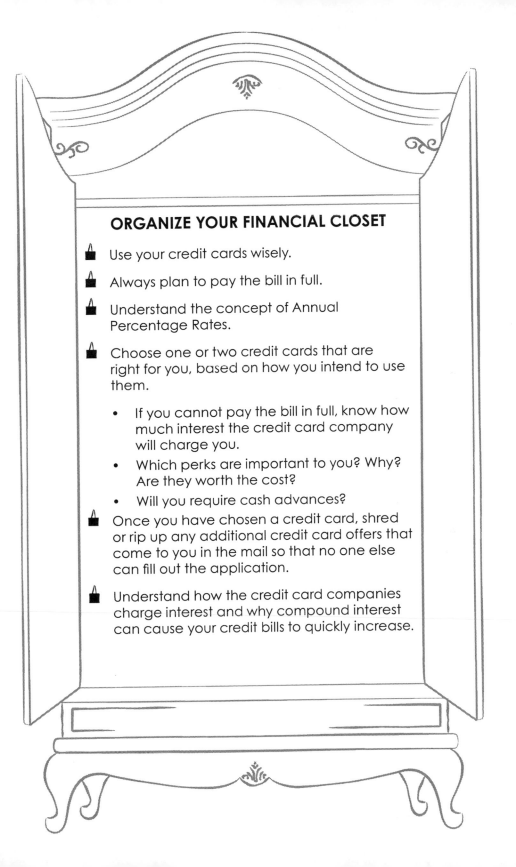

ORGANIZE YOUR FINANCIAL CLOSET

- Use your credit cards wisely.

- Always plan to pay the bill in full.

- Understand the concept of Annual Percentage Rates.

- Choose one or two credit cards that are right for you, based on how you intend to use them.

  - If you cannot pay the bill in full, know how much interest the credit card company will charge you.
  - Which perks are important to you? Why? Are they worth the cost?
  - Will you require cash advances?

- Once you have chosen a credit card, shred or rip up any additional credit card offers that come to you in the mail so that no one else can fill out the application.

- Understand how the credit card companies charge interest and why compound interest can cause your credit bills to quickly increase.

Chapter 8: Interest
SHOES (THEY MULTIPLY)

The first step in dealing with a problem is confessing you have one. Shoes, for example, can be a problem. Like bunnies, they have this tendency to multiply.

Who can help it? Shoes are *so pretty* and you need lots of different kinds: Flats, scuffs, wedgies, ballerinas, kitten-heels, mid-heels, high heels, stilettos, tall boots, short boots, rain boots, pointed toes, round toes,

> **∾ FASHIONISTA FACT: ∾**
> Imelda Marcos, the widow of former dictator Ferdinand Marcos of the Philippines, who was legendary for her shoe collection, once said indignantly, "I did not have 3,000 pairs of shoes. I had 1,060."

blacks, blues, reds, neutrals, which are, of course, different from browns, whites, greens, etc. They come at you from all directions until, suddenly, there is no room left on your closet floor.

Interest can be a lot like shoes. **Interest** is the fee banks pay you either for the privilege of using your money or what you pay banks or credit card companies for the privilege of using their money. When you put your money in a bank, in a savings account or a CD, for example, the bank pays you for keeping your money with them and letting them use it until you ask for it back. In this instance, interest is a good thing. It earns you money. When you use a bank's money (i.e., when you use a credit card and don't pay it off in full), they charge you for using their money. When this happens, the amount of interest you owe can grow quickly and become a major problem—covering the floor of your closet as it were. Get attached to your credit cards, and they will get attached to you.

Regardless of whether the bank pays you or you pay the bank, the concept is the same. For the rest of this chapter, the examples will assume you are using the bank's money and owe the bank. Obviously, if the situation were reversed, instead of you owing the bank, the bank would owe you.

As we've seen, there are two kinds of interest: **Simple** and **compound**. Simple interest means that when you borrow money, you pay back the amount you borrowed, which is called the **principal,** plus the interest. The interest is only calculated on the amount of the principal. The amount of interest you pay back depends on the **interest rate,** which is usually expressed as a percent due for a full year, and the **length of time** over which you borrow the money. There is a formula for calculating simple interest:

> 🛍 *Simple interest equals: Principal multiplied by the interest rate multiplied by the length of time.*

While you don't need to remember the formula, please note two things:

(1) The formula only uses multiplication (not so hard or scary right?) and,

(2) You know what each of the things you need to multiply are.

Here is an example of how to calculate simple interest. If you borrowed one thousand dollars (your principal) at a 10 percent interest rate per year (the bank's fee), for three years (the time period), the simple interest rate is: three hundred dollars (one thousand dollars multiplied by 10 percent interest, multiplied by three years, equals three hundred dollars). The total amount you would owe the bank at the end of the three years would be 1,300 dollars (one thousand dollars, the original amount you borrowed, plus the three hundred dollars interest).

More often, banks and especially credit card companies charge compound interest. **Compound interest** is like simple interest in that when you borrow money, you pay back the amount you borrowed plus the interest. However, unlike with simple interest, where the interest is calculated only once, for compound interest the interest is calculated at the end of each **compounding period**. A compounding period is how often interest is charged—which can be yearly, monthly, weekly, and even daily. This means you are charged interest on the prior period's interest as well as interest on the principal. It's as if your shoes went out and bought their own shoes.

Here is an example of how compound interest is calculated. In the simple interest example above, we borrowed one thousand dollars at a 10 percent interest rate per year for three years. If the bank charged compound interest instead of simple interest, and they were compounding the interest *annually* (once a year), we would use the same formula: Interest equals the Principal multiplied by the Interest Rate multiplied by Length of Time, but we would use it *three times*. The calculation looks like this:

- In year one: one thousand dollars, multiplied by 10 percent, multiplied by one year, equals one hundred dollars. The total amount owed at the end of year one would be 1,100 dollars (one thousand dollars, the original amount you borrowed, plus the interest, one hundred dollars).

- In year two: Perform the calculation again, but this time use as the starting point 1,100 dollars—the balance at the end of year one. To calculate year two, multiply 1,100 dollars by 10 percent by one year. This equals 110 dollars. The total amount owed at the end of year two is 1,210 dollars (one thousand dollars, the original amount you borrowed, plus one hundred dollars, the interest from year one, plus 110 dollars, the interest from year two).

In year three, start with the 1,210 dollars from year two and perform the calculation again: 1,210 dollars multiplied by 10 percent multiplied by one year. The total amount you would owe at the end of year three is 1,331 dollars (one thousand dollars, the original amount you borrowed, plus one hundred dollars, the interest from year one, plus 110 dollars, the interest from year two, plus 121 dollars, the interest from year three).

Remember from example number one, if the interest is calculated using simple interest, at the end of year three, you owe the bank 1,300 dollars. However, if the interest is calculated using compound interest, at the end of year three you owe the bank 1,331 dollars. So over the course of the three years, the difference between the simple and compound interest is thirty-one dollars. No big deal, right?

Well, what happens if the interest rate is 21 percent instead of 10 percent? Twenty-one percent is a more typical interest rate for credit cards. And what would happen if you owed five thousand dollars?

According to a recent study, by Zogby International, almost 20 percent of college students have credit card balances of *at least* five thousand dollars.

Using simple interest at 21 percent, if you took the same three years to pay the five thousand dollars back and did not borrow another penny, you would owe the bank 3,150 dollars in interest, and the total amount you would owe at the end of year three would be 8,150 dollars. Using compound interest, however, the total amount you would owe at the end of year three would be 8,858 dollars. Now the difference between the simple and compound interest calculations is 708 dollars. Adds up, doesn't it?

The higher the interest rate, and the more you borrow, the bigger this difference becomes. Unfortunately for borrowers and credit card users, the interest on most long-term debts and all credit cards is calculated using compound interest. Banks know how much the difference adds up.

To further complicate things, financial institutions charge compound interest in daily, weekly, monthly, or yearly intervals. The shorter the period, the more you owe, because the more frequently the bank performs the calculation. In our example above, I calculated compound interest annually; I performed our calculation once each year for three years. We could have calculated monthly and would have performed the calculation thirty-six times, once a month for three years. Or weekly, we would have performed the calculation 156 times, once a week for three years or, even daily, we would have performed our calculation 1,095 times or once a day for three years. There is a shortcut formula so you do not actually have to perform the calculation that many times:

🔖 Compound interest equals: The principal amount multiplied by (one plus the annual rate divided by the number of time periods)^number of time periods

The ^ symbol means "raised to the power of." At the end of this chapter, there is a mathematical explanation of this formula and the differences between annual, monthly, and daily interest calculations, which you can review if you are interested. For now, trust me and simply understand the concept.

If you purchase big-ticket items, these differences continue to multiply. What happens if you borrow twenty thousand dollars for a car or one hundred thousand dollars on student debt? The principal is larger, the interest payments are larger, and the differences continue to increase. If you miss a payment, what you owe becomes even worse. This is because now you owe additional interest on the principal you did not pay, as well as interest on the interest you did not pay. Understand how much this can hurt when you are trying to pay off a credit card or get out of debt. That's why it is imperative to pay off your debts quickly.

As for your shoe habit, I can't help you. I have a small, tiny shoe problem myself. In fact, quite often I find myself calculating how much something will ultimately cost by how many pairs of shoes I could buy with it.

"She who dies with the most stilettos wins." Nina Garcia

• • •

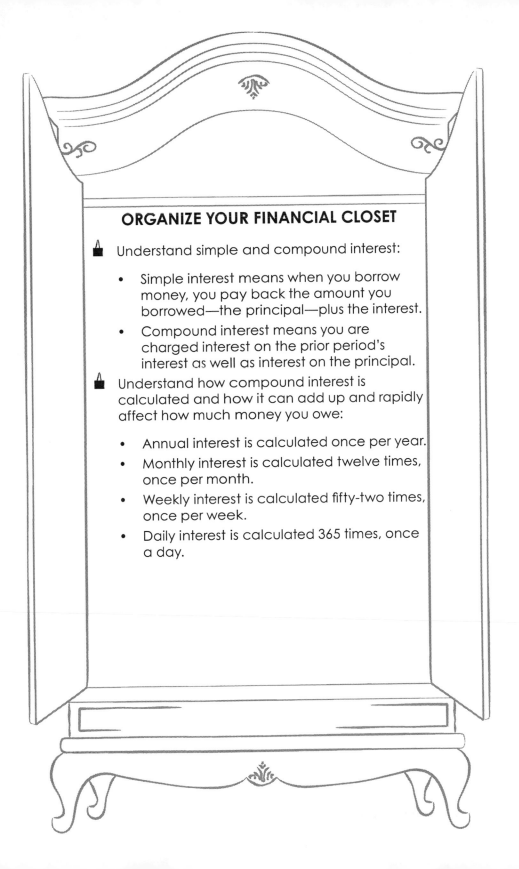

ORGANIZE YOUR FINANCIAL CLOSET

- Understand simple and compound interest:

    - Simple interest means when you borrow money, you pay back the amount you borrowed—the principal—plus the interest.
    - Compound interest means you are charged interest on the prior period's interest as well as interest on the principal.

- Understand how compound interest is calculated and how it can add up and rapidly affect how much money you owe:

    - Annual interest is calculated once per year.
    - Monthly interest is calculated twelve times, once per month.
    - Weekly interest is calculated fifty-two times, once per week.
    - Daily interest is calculated 365 times, once a day.

Advanced compound interest rates

Earlier in the chapter, I showed you a shortcut formula that looks like this:

> 🛍 Compound interest equals: Principal multiplied by (one plus the annual rate divided by the number time periods)^number of time periods

The hat toward the end of the formula (^) is the sign for "raise to the power"—more on that in a minute.

This formula is a shortcut for the formula I provided earlier: Interest equals Principal multiplied by the Interest Rate multiplied by Time. The shortcut enables you to arrive at the answer without doing the calculation so many times. Remember, when you calculate compound interest, you have to do the calculation for each period of time you are paying interest. For example, finding daily compound interest for one year on a certain amount of money would require you to perform the interest rate calculation 365 times. Imagine if you wanted to find the answer for five years. You would have to perform the calculation 1,825 times (365 times five years). Instead, we get to use this nifty shortcut. It looks more complicated than it is.

The only tricky part is you have to use the concept of "raise to the power," which you might not remember from math. **Raise to the power** means you multiply one number (a) by another number (b) by multiplying the first number (a) times itself by (b) times. So, for example, two raised to the power of three (2^3) equals: Two times two times two (2 x 2 x 2), which equals eight (8).

In the compound interest formula, we raise by the number of time periods within a year. One year equals one. One month equals twelve, since there are twelve months in a year. One week equals fifty-two, since there are fifty-two weeks in a year. One day equals 365, because ... that's right. So, for example, the formulas for calculating monthly and daily compound interest are:

- Monthly: Principal (one plus Annual Rate divided by 12)^12
- Daily: Principal (one plus Annual Rate divided by 365)^365

If we borrowed five thousand dollars for one year at 21 percent interest, the difference between the compound interest rate in annual, monthly, weekly, and daily increments looks like this:

Chart 2

CALCULATION FOR ONE YEAR:	ANNUAL	MONTHLY	WEEKLY	DAILY
Total amount of money borrowed (Principal)	$ 5,000	$ 5,000	$ 5,000	$ 5,000
Annual interest rate	21%	21%	21%	21%
Number of time periods (per year)	1	12	52	365
Interest rate per time period	$ 1.210	$ 1.231	$ 1.233	$ 1.234
Total interest	$ 1,050	$ 1,157	$ 1,166	$ 1,168
Total principal + interest	$ 6,050	$ 6,157	$ 6,166	$ 6,168
Difference between annual and daily interest	$ 118			

In this example, paying daily interest would cost you 118 dollars more than paying annual interest

As you can see, you pay the least amount of interest if the interest is compounded yearly ($1,050) and the most interest if the interest is compounded daily ($1,168). While 118 dollars may not seem like a lot of money, remember the difference gets larger the more you borrow and the longer you take to pay it back.

• • •

Chapter 9: Time Value Of Money
IT'S IN STYLE TODAY (WILL IT BE TOMORROW?)

What's hot? What's new? What's now? What to buy? Keep? Store? Fashionistas want things now, today, while they're in style. Fashionistas measure time in seasons and hate to wait. For example, would you rather have one thousand dollars today or one thousand dollars three years from now? I'm going to assume you answered today. After all, why wait three years?

By expressing your preference for having one thousand dollars now, you get the concept that, all things being equal, it is better to get money sooner rather than later and proved that you already understand the basic concept of the **time value of money**. But do you know why? Isn't the one thousand dollars you receive today worth the same as the one thousand dollars you would get in three years?

Actually, no, it's not. Why? You can invest it and earn a profit on it or at least earn interest on it:

> ∾ **FASHIONISTA FACT:** ∾
>
> When buying jewelry, remember the description does not always reflect time or value: Antique jewelry has to be more than one hundred years old whereas vintage jewelry simply has to be anywhere between ten years and who-knows-how-many years old. Estate jewelry has to have been sold previously—regardless of when.

- One thousand dollars invested today, for three years, at 10 percent interest will equal 1,300 dollars.
- One thousand dollars obtained three years from now equals one thousand dollars.
- So, in this scenario, the difference between the two equals three hundred dollars.

But there's more to the story than that. The value of the one thousand dollars in three years would actually be arrived at by calculating compound interest:

- One thousand dollars invested for one year at 10 percent interest will equal 1,100 dollars.
- 1,100 dollars invested at 10 percent interest for one year will equal 1,210 dollars.
- 1,210 dollars invested at 10 percent interest for one year will equal 1,331 dollars.
- So in this example, the actual difference between one thousand dollars invested today and one thousand dollars invested in three years equals 331 dollars.

This idea forms a core principle of finance. *If you can earn interest on your money, that money is worth more to you now than it is to you later.* And the more interest you can earn on your money, the truer this becomes.

You know from Chapter Five that money deposited in a savings account will earn some interest and that money in a CD will earn more interest. And you will learn in Chapter Eleven that money invested in stocks or other financial instruments—or real estate—has the potential to earn even more. Because money has the ability to multiply itself, thereby creating more money for you over time, it's better to receive money today, so you can put it to use, than in the future.

Many real life financial problems involve **cash flows** that occur at different points of time. For example, when you make an investment, you receive the interest on it over some period of time— months or years. Likewise, when you pay off a debt,

∾ **FASHIONISTA FACT:** ∾

According to *In Style Secrets of Style*, vintage items that are as in style today as they were in the past, and will be in the future, include: Mary Quant minis, Yves St. Laurent tuxedos, Halston jersey dresses, DVF wrap dresses (from the first time around), sheath dresses by Christian Dior, Coco Chanel, or Hubert de Givenchy, trench coats by Burberry or Aquascutum, accessories from venerable design houses such as Gucci, Louis Vuitton, Hermes, Chanel, Prada, and Bottega Veneta.

unless you pay it all off at once, you pay it over some period of time. The real value and/or cost of these different cash flows take into consideration the time value of money. The money you make, earn, or spend today has a different value than the money you make, earn, or spend in the future. For example, if you received five thousand dollars five years from now, versus receiving one thousand dollars a year for five years, and you invested the one thousand dollars each year, earning 10 percent interest per year, you would wind up with 1,716 dollars more:

- Year 1: One thousand dollars invested for one year at 10 percent interest equals 1,100 dollars, as we've seen
- Year 2: One thousand dollars plus the 1,100 dollars from year one at 10 percent interest equals 2,310 dollars
- Year 3: One thousand dollars plus the 2,310 dollars from year two at 10 percent interest equals 3,641 dollars
- Year 4: One thousand dollars plus the 3,641 dollars from year three at 10 percent interest equals 5,105 dollars
- Year 5: One thousand dollars plus the 5,105 dollars from year four at 10 percent interest equals 6,716 dollars total (yea for you)

But of course, the same holds true if you spend the money. If you spent one thousand dollars a year for five years rather than waiting to spend all five thousand dollars at the end of year five, in fact you would have spent the equivalent of 6,716 dollars because, had you invested the money, you would have the interest to spend also.

At first glance, this may seem to contradict what I said about always paying off credit cards. The reason it doesn't is that the compound interest the credit card companies charge when you don't pay your bill in full is almost always much higher than the interest you can earn from saving or investing. In addition, since the credit card companies charge daily compound interest on your interest, you end up owing more, faster, than you can earn.

There is one other concept you should be aware of. Since you have a finite amount of money about which to make decisions, you need to think about the **opportunity cost** that is involved—that is, what you might be giving up with each decision you make. Every decision has consequences. So consider what something is really costing you—today and in the future. The good news is that opportunity cost is not really a number, so no math. Rather, it is a set of alternatives. For example, if you stay in a less-than-fulfilling relationship, you may be giving up the opportunity to meet a new, more compatible person. And, obviously, if you purchase an outfit at Juicy Couture, unless you have an unlimited shopping budget, you give up the opportunity to purchase something even cuter at Urban Outfitters. In finance, opportunity cost refers to the price you may pay in lost opportunities by choosing one alternative over another. So it behooves you to think about the opportunity cost as you weigh decisions.

As a Fashionista you think about this every day. If I skip dinner for a week or two to pay for those boots, will I be too wiped-out to enjoy wearing them? If I skip on cosmetics to support my Starbucks habit, will I drink my coffee alone? If I use my rent money to buy a whole new wardrobe, will I have a closet to put it in? Opportunity costs loom large in such decisions.

• • •

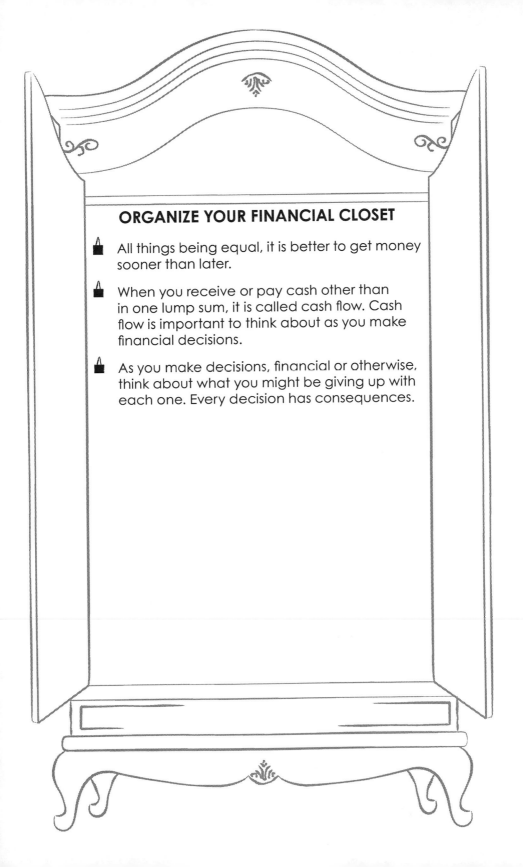

ORGANIZE YOUR FINANCIAL CLOSET

- All things being equal, it is better to get money sooner than later.

- When you receive or pay cash other than in one lump sum, it is called cash flow. Cash flow is important to think about as you make financial decisions.

- As you make decisions, financial or otherwise, think about what you might be giving up with each one. Every decision has consequences.

Chapter 10: Debt
TRENDY SPLURGES (DO YOU REALLY NEED IT?)

Fashions come and go but debt is never stylish. Whether your style is classic, couture, casual, cutting edge, or *au courant*, debt will never look flattering on you. What exactly is debt? Simply put, debt is owing money. Remember in Chapter Seven when your friend bought you that cappuccino? You were in debt to her for five dollars. Want to buy something you can't afford, like another little black dress for the season? Unpaid credit card bills are debt. Yes, I know your credit cards jumped out of your purse and did a little jig at the cash register, and, yes, that LBD was unbelievable. But if you couldn't pay for it at the time, you probably should not have bought it. It put you in debt. Want to finance a car? A lease is debt. Want to get an education? Student loans are debt. Want to buy a house? Mortgage is debt. Whether you owe five dollars or one hundred thousand dollars, and regardless what it's for, if you have borrowed money, you are in debt.

Debt is worse than wearing something you really regretted...and having the pictures to prove it.

"Okay, so I'm in debt!" Yes, you probably are. Of course, not every single one of you is in debt right this minute. But at some point in your life, you will be. While all debt is money you owe, not all of the kinds of debts listed above are the same. Just like there are good trends and bad trends, there is such a thing as **good debt** and **bad debt**. Not all debts are created equal.

Guess which of the things listed above is a **bad debt**? You got it. The LBD. Yes, it looks amazing on you, but if you can't afford it, then you need to exercise some discipline and not buy it. Did you know the car lease in my example above is usually not considered good debt? Cars leases and loans are usually not considered good debt because cars do not go up in value. In fact, their value decreases as soon as you drive off the lot—every day they are older and worth a little less. However, if you need to buy or lease a car on credit for work or school, and you make sure you choose the least expensive car you can afford, that's considered pretty good debt.

There is another reason credit card debt and cars are not considered good debt: You cannot deduct a portion of the interest you paid from your income taxes. Taxes are discussed in Chapter Fifteen, but for now you should know that the government rewards you by letting you deduct a portion of your interest from good debt— student loans and houses—from your taxes. The more you deduct, the less tax you pay, and the more money you have left over. The government knows bad debt is bad for you and so you cannot deduct interest from bad debt—credit cards and cars—from your taxes.

A college or graduate school education and a home are sometimes considered **good debt** because, although you had to borrow money to pay for them, you have something of value after you have paid back what you owe, interest and all. Even more importantly, the value of what you have may go up. A college education is price-less. In 2006, people with associates degrees (two years of college) earned on average eight thousand dollars a year more than people with a high school diploma, and people with bachelors degrees (four years of col-lege) earned on average seventy-three thousand dollars a year more than people with a high school diploma. An education provides you with a career, and a career is the most valuable thing you will ever have, other than your friends and family. It is how you will earn money and sup-port yourself. Without a career, you can't really survive on your own. If you are reading this book, you are planning on taking control of your finances rather than mooching off your family or putting up with the demands of a "spe-cial friend." Being educated is always fashionable. And if you have to go into debt to get educated—do it.

One way to keep your education costs low is by starting out at a community college for the first year or two and then transferring to a higher priced, more prestigious school for the last two or three years.

A home is a second example of good debt. Homes are considered good debt because houses often go up in value—although not always. Mortgage problems can be created when under-qualified people put very little money down and get in over their heads, and when banks make bad deals by loaning money when they shouldn't. Homes are also considered good debt because you can deduct a portion of your mortgage interest from your taxes. When you purchase a home, you pay a down payment, a certain amount of money up front, and borrow the rest. As you pay back your loan, a portion of your payment is applied to the principal—the original amount you borrowed—to reduce the amount you owe the bank. The rest of the payment—the interest on the principal—the bank keeps as payment for letting you use the bank's money. The more payments you make, the lower your principal gets. The lower the principal gets the less interest you owe on it. Since you will likely pay the same amount every month, more and more of your payment goes toward paying down principal in a "virtuous cycle." Once you have paid off your loan, you own your house. If its value goes up, you will own a house worth more than what you paid for it. If the house goes down in value, the reverse is true. If you sell the house before you pay off the loan in full, you get to keep whatever the difference is between the sales price and what you owe.

Whether the debt is good or bad, if you owe it, you need to pay it back. This is where people often get themselves into trouble. How do you keep yourself out of trouble? One of the main things you can do is to read and understand what you are agreeing to before you sign any documents (such as credit card agreements, car loans, or mortgages). If someone tries to rush you into signing, it probably means they don't want you to understand what you are agreeing to be responsible for. Don't let them have their way with you. Read the documents and find out:

Not all loans operate this way. There are a lot of different kinds, such as interest only and balloon. In an interest only loan, when you make your payment, you only pay the interest you owe. You do not contribute to the principal or build your equity, but your monthly payments are lower than in a traditional loan. In a balloon loan, there are low interest rate payments and then one large payment at the end of the loan. You need to research the different kinds of loans very carefully and work with a real estate professional if you are considering buying a house or condo.

- What interest rate are you being charged?
- How is the interest going to be calculated?
- What happens if you are late with a payment?
- Are there penalties if you pay off your debt early?

What do you do if you find yourself with a lot of unstylish debt you know you can't pay back?

- First, stop, absolutely stop, using your credit cards. Find a way to live within your means. Go back and re-read Chapter One, on budgeting.

- Second, pay off your credit card debt. If your credit card debt is the debt you can't pay, you can often work with the credit card company to set up a payment plan or to reduce your interest rates. If your credit card company won't help you, you can call a reputable credit counselor for assistance. Often, they will work with your credit card company and other companies you owe money to and can help reduce what you owe. Log onto www.consumercredit. com for assistance finding a credit counselor who can help you.

- Third, if you have many types of the same kind of loans, consolidate. Consolidation means you group all of your similar loans together with just one company. For example, you can get a student consolidation loan where you combine multiple student loans and pay a fixed interest rate to just one company. Or you can combine all of your credit card balances onto one single card (with a lower rate than those you have) that you pay off on a regular basis.

- Fourth, beware of scams. There are a lot of con artists who prey on people desperate to solve their credit problems. They may offer to get your debt "suspended" or "canceled" if you pay their fees in advance, sell you supposed credit protection, or offer to help you re-build your credit. These kinds of offers can be very tempting, especially when you are vulnerable. Remember, if it sounds too good to be true, it probably is. Keep in mind that saying about free lunches, as in, there's no such thing.

The most crucial thing to learn about debt—after the number one rule, which is don't incur it—is that you should always take it seriously. Wasting it on something frivolous does not become a true Fashionista. A true Fashionista searches out the highest style, but only at a price she can afford.

∾ FASHIONISTA FACT: ∾

When design intoxication hits and you find yourself with a shopping hangover, remind yourself that debt is not stylish and the financially responsible thing to do is return the items if still possible. Your head and your bank account will thank you.

- Alcohol hangover: Mild to excruciating headache and queasy stomach, usually gone by mid-day. Costs include price of cocktails, lots of empty calories, and possible loss of self-esteem.

- Shopping hangover: Mild headache and intermittent cringing, which can take days or months to recover from—depending on the size of the bill. Costs include debt from purchase of designer items, interest fees and late charges from credit card bill, and possible loss of self-esteem.

Credit scores

A **credit score,** also known as a FICO score, is a particular calculation of your credit history that measures your trustworthiness to lenders. It is a number that credit-givers, such as credit card companies and car dealers, use to help them decide if they want to loan you money, by answering the following questions: Can they expect you to be able to pay them back as agreed, and what are the odds you won't pay them back at all? What amount do they feel comfortable loaning you? How much do they want to charge you? The less confidence they have that they will be paid back, the more interest they will charge you.

In Fashionista terms, a credit score can be the difference between being granted VIP status or being shown the door at your favorite store or club. A credit score tracks whether you are more likely to be a good customer or a bad customer.

Think of your favorite store. If you visit it frequently, are nice to the staff, are enthusiastic about their merchandise, and avoid bad behavior such as shoplifting or always trying to pay less than retail, they will love you. They'll put you on their VIP list, you'll get first dibs on new selection, sales, and discounts, they'll call you ahead of time to let you know your favorites are in stock, and in many other ways they will take extra special care of you. On the other hand, if you're a complainer who's rude to the staff, reluctant to pay retail, and constantly return items for no good reason, you're unlikely to be welcome and, in fact, will probably be discouraged from coming at all. The golden rule works here: Treat the stores the way you want to be treated, and the good karma will come back to you.

You can guess where I'm going with this. The more you respect your credit score, the more lenders respect you in return. This becomes really important when you suddenly have some big-ticket items you're thinking about buying.

Your credit score is a number that is assigned to you by a credit agency; it is a snapshot of the credit risk they judge you to be at a particular point in time. Credit scores range from 300, indicating you're a poor risk, to 850, indicating you're a great risk and will be offered the best deals.

When you borrow money or apply for a credit card, you typically go to a bank or credit card company, which will immediately look at your credit score. How much money did you earn, and how much did you spend? How responsible were you? Did you honor your commitments and pay your bills on time? What is your current net worth? The more responsible you have been financially, the higher your score. And a high credit score means that you will be allowed to borrow more money at a lower interest rate than a person who has a lower credit score.

So if you've got a great credit score, you can buy your car or your house more cheaply than can someone whose credit score is lower. Why? Because you will pay less interest. Less interest is your reward for having built up such a respectable credit score. (With the money you save on interest you'll have more left over for other things, such as designer clothes and footwear.)

Credit scores take the subjectivity out of the bank's decision whether or not to loan you money. They focus on the inner financial you; race, age, looks, etc. are not part of the equation. Only your good or bad financial position at the time counts.

How do you know what your score is? Your credit score is calculated by a **credit agency,** a company that collects information about you on behalf of lenders. They get their information from companies who have previously loaned you money. Credit card companies, cell phone companies, department stores, car companies, etc., all provide information about you to the credit agencies. The credit agencies then give this information to lenders and credit *card* companies (which are different from credit agencies) so they in turn can determine if they want to loan you money. How much of a loan risk are you? How much are you good for—what dollar amount—and what interest rate should they charge you? Your behavior over time is all that they are judging you by. Kind of gives you pause, doesn't it? Who knew that a couple of bills mailed in late or a few too many splurges racked up on one card could cost you real money down the line?

Here's how: To calculate your credit score, credit agencies look at how you have conducted yourself over the last seven years, in five specific areas:

1. Late payments. How often were you late paying your bills?
2. Frequency and patterns of credit use. How often do you use your credit cards and what do you buy with them? How much money do you have outstanding on your accounts?
3. How long have you had credit?
4. How many times have they been asked about your credit? Companies ask about your credit when you do things like sign up for a cell phone contract or apply for an apartment, credit card, car or student loan.
5. What types of credit do you have? Do you have different kinds such as credit card *and* a car loan or a mortgage? Lenders are kind of like men— the more you have, the more they want you for themselves!

Each of these five factors carries different weight:

1. Approximately 35 percent of your score is based on your payment history. It is worse to have a recent late payment than a late payment that occurred over twelve months ago. A recent late payment can lower your score by sixty points or more, which gives you another reason to pay your bills on time and not overspend if you can possibly help it.

2. Approximately 30 percent is based on your existing debt. How maxed out are you? Try not to go over 50 percent of the maximum limit on any credit cards you have. If you are over 50 percent on any card, consider switching to spread your debt among other cards, and, better yet, don't buy another thing until you are below 50 percent. And, of course, ideally you should not have credit card debt at all because you only buy on credit what you can pay off during the same month.

3. Approximately 15 percent is based on how long your credit has been established. Do not close accounts that have been open for at least three years and on which you have a perfect payment history. These cards have a positive effect on your credit score.

4. Approximately 10 percent is based on inquiries. The more inquires that have been made about you, the lower your credit score. However,

some inquiries that happen close together do not count. For example, if you are buying a car and you visit a couple of different dealers and each one calls the credit agencies about you, the calls count as one inquiry in total. This is also true for mortgage and insurance industry inquiries.

5. Approximately 10 percent is based on type of credit. A combination of credit types is best. For example, a mortgage, an auto loan, and a credit card or two is ideal. Ten different department store credit cards is not ideal.

To find out your score, call any one of the three **credit agencies** listed below and ask for your credit report. By law, you are entitled to one free credit report per year. If you want to check it more than once a year, like when you are purchasing something big, then you'll pay a low fee to get a second report.

- Equifax: www.equifax.com (800-685-1111)
- Experian: www.experian.com (888-EXPERIAN)
- Trans Union: www.transunion.com (800-916-8800)

So how do you maintain VIP status with your credit score? Review the five factors the credit agencies use to score you and try to maximize your points in each category. Pay your bills on time. Have at least one credit card, buy a little with it every month, and then pay the bill in full. If you have debts, pay them down or off. It might take effort and time to improve your score, but it can be done.

• • •

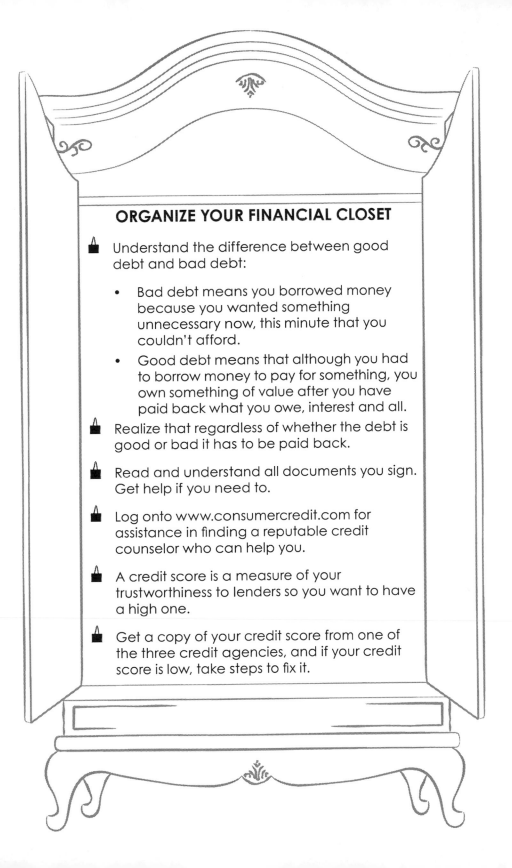

ORGANIZE YOUR FINANCIAL CLOSET

- Understand the difference between good debt and bad debt:

    - Bad debt means you borrowed money because you wanted something unnecessary now, this minute that you couldn't afford.
    - Good debt means that although you had to borrow money to pay for something, you own something of value after you have paid back what you owe, interest and all.

- Realize that regardless of whether the debt is good or bad it has to be paid back.

- Read and understand all documents you sign. Get help if you need to.

- Log onto www.consumercredit.com for assistance in finding a reputable credit counselor who can help you.

- A credit score is a measure of your trustworthiness to lenders so you want to have a high one.

- Get a copy of your credit score from one of the three credit agencies, and if your credit score is low, take steps to fix it.

Chapter 11: Investments

WHAT'S THE EVENT? (DIFFERENT OCCASIONS CALL FOR DIFFERENT STYLES)

Fill in the blank. You *would* wear [this item] to [this event]. You *wouldn't* wear [this item] to [this event]. Just as you need different clothes for different occasions, you need to invest your money in different ways for different reasons.

When you put your money in the bank, whether you put it in a checking or savings account, you are keeping it as **cash**. Checking and savings accounts are great places to keep cash. They pay you interest on your money and, if you don't take any money out of your account, the amount of money you have slowly increases because the interest adds up and, if it's compound, you start earning interest on your interest. But you are still not necessarily earning as much from your money as you could be. Your money can work harder for you.

One way to describe this increase in value is through a concept called **return on investment**, a measurement of how much your money has

Yes, I'm repeating myself, but let me say again that the best way to make your money work harder is to pay off your credit card debt. This will give you a guaranteed 20 percent return on the amount of money you owed—more if your credit card has higher than 20 percent interest—because the interest rate is what the outstanding balance is costing you each month.

increased or decreased over a one-year time period relative to what you invested. In a checking or savings account your return comes from the interest the bank pays you. Of course, there are lots of other kinds of investments that also could go up in value. Most of these investments will help you earn more on your money than you can earn from simply being paid interest by a bank. But beware, because as we all know, there is no such thing as a free lunch. A higher return on investment almost always comes with a higher risk of losing your money.

> If something sounds too good to be true, it probably is.

The names for some common investments are **stocks, bonds, mutual funds, index funds**. To browse through them may require you to wander into a whole new department of your financial store, but it will be well worth your while to do so before deciding which, if any, of them to buy.

What is a stock? What is a bond? What are mutual and index funds? And why do you care? Let's begin with why you should care. Purchasing stocks, bonds, or mutual funds can allow your money to grow, and grow faster, than it will if you simply leave it in your checking or savings account—and obviously that's a good thing.

There is a downside, of course, or everyone would do it. Although you can earn more money, there is no guarantee you will. Unfortunately, you can also lose money—a lot of money. So the central thing to think about before purchasing anything more complicated than a bank CD, which is insured against losses, is whether or not you can afford to take any risk at all with your money and, if you feel you can do so in hopes of better returns, then how much of a risk you can afford to take. Risk tolerance is different for everyone—think sweater-set, pencil skirt, and ballet flats versus chains, leather, and platforms. You need to choose what is comfortable to you.

Buying **stock** is buying ownership in an individual company; how much ownership depends on how much stock you buy. When you buy a share of stock, you are buying a small piece of everything the company owns and owes. So, for example, if a stock is selling for 110 dollars per share and you ask your stockbroker to purchase 110 dollars worth, you now own one share of the company. If the company has one hundred thousand total shares outstanding, you just bought .00001 percent of the company.

> ∾ **FASHIONISTA FACT:** ∾
> In medieval times ballet flats were popular with both men and women. They went out of fashion in the seventeenth and eighteenth centuries when the high-heeled shoe took over. High heels quickly went out of style, though, after Marie Antoinette allegedly walked to the guillotine wearing a pair, and functional shoes prevailed in the 1800s. Ballet flats did not return to popularity until the 1950s when Brigitte Bardot wore a pair in *And God Created Woman* and Audrey Hepburn wore them with skinny jeans in *Funny Face*.

Stocks are traded on a stock market. You buy stocks with the help of a stockbroker who is sort of like a personal shopper for stocks. There are well over 2,500 different companies whose stocks are traded on the New York Stock Exchange (NYSE) alone.

Companies earn money and lose money. As their fortunes go, so does their stock. By owning their stock, you can make or lose money right along with them. Examples of the different kinds of familiar retail stocks you could own are: Abercrombie & Fitch, Saks, Nike, Ralph Lauren. Not only can you own a piece of these companies but you can show your brand loyalty by wearing them. Peter Lynch, a famous investor, once said, "If you like the store, chances are you'll like the stock."

Peter Lynch also said, "You should invest in companies you understand."

Think of a **stock market** as resembling a department store where you can buy all sorts of designer clothes, cosmetics, shoes, and bags in one place. In the stock market, you can buy stocks and bonds and other financial instruments instead. In the United States, there are two main markets: The New York Stock Exchange (NYSE) and the National Association of Securities Dealers Automated Quotations (NASDAQ). Internationally, there are lots of others, like the London Stock Exchange and the Hong Kong Stock Exchange. You can shop at these markets just like you can at any other market, as long as you use your broker or have an investment account that will let you purchase directly.

Each market (or exchange) lists all of the stocks and other financial instruments it sells. You can browse all the offerings, narrow down your selections, and hone in on your purchases. You can even try on, before you buy, by selecting a stock to watch. Don't spend any money until after you have watched it for a while and also learned something about the company. See how much it fluctuates; the price of stocks constantly changes and you have to be sure that the stock you are watching is a value at the price at which you decide to buy it. If the shoes were a steal at 125 dollars, would you still think they were worth buying at two hundred dollars?

I do not recommend owning individual stocks unless you *really* know what you are doing and can afford to lose some money. Particularly when you are starting out, it is much better to own a professionally managed **mutual fund** or, even better, an **exchange traded or**

> ~ **FASHIONISTA FACT:** ~
> Founded in 1830, the oldest department store in the world is Austin's, in Derry, Northern Ireland. The model for what we now think of as a department store was Le Bon Marche in Paris, France. Originally opened in 1832 by Aristide Boucicaut, Le Bon Marche offered a wide variety of goods in different "departments" under one roof at a fixed price, no haggling or bargaining, and a money-back guarantee allowing exchanges and refunds. There was also a restaurant so you could eat while you shopped.

index fund (see page 118), which uses a different kind of shopping approach than that of buying stocks.

A bond is a loan to a company or to a government. When you buy a bond, you agree to loan your money to the company or government in exchange for interest payments they make to you and the return of your money at a later set date. You receive your interest rate payments in the form of checks, sent out within a set time frame. You receive the full amount of your original loan back when the loan matures. The interest rate you receive depends on how strong the company is. The stronger the company, the less risky the loan and therefore the less interest you receive. (Conversely, the weaker the company, the riskier the loan and the more interest you receive.) Just as you have a credit score, so do companies and governments. Like you, the better their score, the lower interest rate they have to pay. Where are bonds traded? Just as there is a stock market, so there is a bond market. However, unlike stocks, some bonds don't have to be traded in the market. When bonds are not sold on the bond market the transaction is called **Over the Counter (OTC)**.

A **mutual fund** lets people who have the same financial goals and objectives pool their money together to buy small pieces of lots of different companies simultaneously, as a group. Mutual funds purchase a variety of stocks and/or bonds. Unlike stocks or bonds, which are separate entities, a mutual fund can contain both stocks and bonds. When you buy into a mutual fund, you buy a share of the fund, just as you buy a share of a company when you buy a stock, but in this instance you own a share of the mutual fund—that is, a share of all of the stocks and bonds the group has purchased—rather than of one individual company. Why would you invest in a mutual fund instead of a stock or a bond? Because mutual funds are able to take advantage of their size (buying power) to charge much lower commission rates than you pay when you buy stocks and bonds on your own, which can save you a lot of money over time. A second reason is a concept called **diversification**. You wouldn't want to stock your closet only with feather boas—or even with jeans and tees—would you? Of course not. Diversification means your money is spread around different types of investments, in different kinds of companies, which will minimize your risk. If one of the companies in the fund has a bad season—orange turns out not to be the new black—odds are that another company in the fund will balance it out by having a good season—black is once again the new black.

∾ FASHIONISTA FACT: ∾

"_____ is the new black" started with the legendary *Vogue* editor Diana Vreeland in 1962, when she observed that "shocking pink is the navy blue of India." Vreeland was commenting on the copious use of pink as the base color for much of the attire in India, much like navy blue at that time was the core color of most outfits in New York City. In the late 1970s the expression changed to "X is the new neutral," which morphed in the 1980s to "X is the new black."

Mutual funds have a **fund manager** (again, think personal shopper), who manages the fund by picking the stocks and bonds for it. The manager's trades can cost you less money in commissions than you would pay if you traded individual stocks and bonds yourself. Many charge different kinds of fees to invest in them so you need to look at all of the charges and how they're levied before selecting a mutual fund.

Another kind of investment is an **exchange traded** or **index fund,** a type of mutual fund, which has no fund manager. Instead, an index fund seeks to match the performance of the overall **stock market** or a portion of the overall stock market by holding all of the securities in the index, in the same proportions as the index or by statistically sampling the market and holding "representative" securities. For the beginning investor, an index fund is often the best way to go. You purchase an index fund through a broker, but since there is no fund manager, you pay lower commission than you do to purchase a mutual fund. Since an index fund seeks to match the performance of the market, in a sense you are betting the market will go up. When it does, your index fund goes up with it. However, when the market goes down, your index fund will go down, too. But since you are betting on a much larger pool (the whole market) instead of betting on one company (a stock) or several companies (a mutual fund) you are spreading your risk.

> Hemlines fluctuate between micro-mini and trains depending on designers' collective will. Like skirt lengths, the financial markets have proven to be subject to the same kind of whims. In fact, in the 1920s, the economist George Taylor conceived the hemline index, finding that skirts got longer as the economy slowed. There's also been talk of a haircut index with a change in style to short locks signaling a declining economy.

Yet another kind of investment is a **401K**, which is a retirement plan your employer can offer you if they so desire. It's not something you purchase separately, like a stock or a mutual fund. You can only get a 401K through your employer. A 401K automatically takes money out of your paycheck—you decide how much, up to the federal limit—and deposits it into a retirement savings account set up for you. You then decide, based on the options the employer provides, how your retirement account will invest your money. Usually your employer will offer a range of choices, ranging in risk from preppie conservative to cutting-edge fashionista.

The money you allow your company to deduct from your paycheck and put in your 401K is deducted pre-tax, meaning before you pay taxes on it. In other words, you do not have to pay any taxes on the money you put in. You get to invest this part of your paycheck, earn money on the government's share of its taxes (see Chapter 15), and keep the money you earned on that share when you eventually withdraw the money from your account and pay the taxes on the amount you withdraw. So you have the use of the government's money to earn interest until you are sixty-five or older and can withdraw the money.

If your employer offers a 401K plan you should take full advantage of it. It will force you to save because it takes money out of your paycheck before you ever see it. Plus, it will lower your tax rate, since it is money you won't be taxed on, and, even better, some employers offer you an incentive to invest in a 401K by contributing to your account as well, which should make participating irresistible.

The amount your employer contributes is called a **matching contribution** and usually consists of a percentage of your paycheck up to a defined maximum. For example, an employer might offer to match you fifty cents for every dollar you contribute up to some specific percentage of your salary, usually three or four percent. So over the course of a year, if you invested one thousand dollars, your employer would deposit five hundred dollars into your account. This is like getting an instant raise with no extra duties required.

If you leave the company, you can take the 401K account with you and roll it over into an **Individual Retirement Account** (IRA), a kind of stand-alone 401K, or leave it with your former employer to administer even after you leave. Sometimes they charge you a fee for doing this so I suggest rolling it over into an IRA. (Also, if you plan to have more than one employer before you are sixty-five, it is nice to keep your accounts together in one place that you control.) IRAs are more flexible than a 401K; your money can be invested in whatever you want, not just what your employer has chosen—from stocks and mutual funds to bonds and real estate. There are lots of different kinds of IRAs so you need to check them all out. The downside of IRAs is there is a limit on the amount you can invest in them each year, although 401K rollovers are exempt from this limitation. The limit changes so you need to look up the limit for a particular year. You can Google "IRA" to learn more.

There is also a special IRA called a **Roth IRA**. Roth IRAs have lots of rules, but if you follow them, any money you put into one is taxed at that time and even if it grows, you won't have to pay any more taxes on it. For example, if your account doubled in value over the years, even when you cash out at retirement, you'd get half the money tax-free.

Buying any financial investment has risk associated with it. In general, individual stocks are riskier than index funds, mutual funds, and bonds. Mutual funds are riskier than index funds and bonds. Index funds are riskier than bonds. And they are all usually riskier than cash. However, remember, cash does not grow, so by keeping all of your money in cash your money is not working for you. Further, within each type of investment there are different levels of risk. Some stocks are obviously a lot riskier than others. For example, if you had purchased one share of Revlon in October 2003, five years later you would have lost approximately 54 percent of your money. But if you purchased Estee Lauder, you would have gained more than 10 percent over the same time period. Similarly, some bonds are riskier than others and some mutual funds are riskier than others. You get the idea.

To backtrack a little, we should discuss how you actually buy these kinds of investments. To invest in a CD, you go to a bank. To invest in a stock, bond, or mutual or index fund, you open a kind of bank account called an investment **brokerage account**. Like a checking account and a savings account, a brokerage account is held at a financial institution that is a lot like a bank. However, unlike a checking or savings account, you don't usually use a brokerage account to write checks, pay your bills, or withdraw cash when you need it. A brokerage account has a different function: It allows you to purchase and keep stocks, bonds, mutual funds, and other types of financial investments (kind of like a closet for your investments). You add or subtract to your financial closet by using a professional called a **broker**. A broker can help you choose investments and buy them for you, or just buy what you've already chosen. They are a bit like stylists: They can help you find just the right item, but you do have to be careful since their taste does not always match yours.

For their services, brokers charge you a fee for their services, which is called a **commission** or **commission rate**. Their fees can range from as low as five dollars to upwards of several hundred dollars for each purchase, depending on how much they help you, how much you spend, and what you buy. Just as you get a discount at a sale, there are also brokers called **discount brokers**, who will give you a discount off their fee. Discount brokers charge you less than regular brokers simply to make transactions, but they will not give you advice. Their job is to purchase for you. So they are best suited to people who know what they are doing or who have done their homework thoroughly.

Brokers also often help you look up information about investments you are interested in and keep you informed. You want to stay current about the investments you purchase and the stock market in general, since market conditions and stock prices can be very volatile. Reading the reports brokers offer is a great way to start learning. They can provide general market information, in-depth analysis on various subjects, and reports on individual companies.

HOW TO SELECT A BROKER

Some examples of brokers include "Traditional" or "Full Service": Goldman Sachs and Morgan Stanley; "Discount": Ameritrade and TD Waterhouse; "Both": Charles Schwab and Merrill Lynch

Check out their websites, keeping in mind the following questions:

- How much help do I want or need? If you are confident about what you want to buy, and how best to make a decision, go for a discount broker. If you want to bounce your ideas off a professional, find a full-service broker.

- Commissions: How and how much do they charge for their services? Every dollar you pay is a dollar less to invest or shop with. You need to ask specific questions and check out their website.
- Also take note of how accessible their website is. Is it easy to follow? Do you like the feel of it? Is it clear?
- Are there minimum opening balance requirements or fees for maintaining the account? Some accounts require a minimum—do you have it and do you want to commit to keeping that money in the account? Do you have to pay a fee? How much? How often?

To learn more about brokers and how to find one, Google "brokerage account." There are also lots of websites on the Internet offering beginners an opportunity to learn more about investing. The Investment FAQ is a good one; so is About.com. Check out a few different websites until you feel comfortable with one.

We still need to discuss one final concept: **Asset allocation**. Asset allocation is a reference to how much of your money to put into each of a variety of investments. You need a balanced financial closet so that you don't find yourself in effect with all tops and no bottoms. It is a good idea to keep your money in different places: Cash, stocks, bonds, houses, cars, etc. You will hear people talk about allocating assets in percentages. For example they—now you—will say things like, "I have 15 percent of my assets in cash." The rest might be in their house, car, stocks, etc. Think shoes. Much as you may love them, it makes a lot more sense to allocate only 15 percent of your total closet to them than, say, 100 percent. You would no doubt have a fabulous shoe collection but nothing to wear with them. Point made.

If you are just starting out, keep in mind that not knowing where or how to invest your extra money is a high-class problem to have. It is my hope you will save your money, review the basics I have covered here, and continue to learn so your money will increase.

WHAT TO SAVE AT EVERY AGE

Once you have opened an account and deposited a check, you can start investing your money, after completing your homework by doing a lot of research. Remember to check out index funds first. Your broker can help you investigate different investments, you can read books, surf the web, and talk to everyone you know.

Your investment choices will depend upon how old you are, how much money you have in your savings account, how much debt you have, what your goals are, and how much risk you are comfortable with. That being said, there are some guidelines to consider. There is no right answer, but a general rule of thumb is 100 percent minus your age equals the percent you have invested in stocks.

- 20s: You can afford to take risks. In the event your investments have problems and you lose money, you have plenty of time to earn it back. Of your total savings, roughly 80 percent of your savings should be in stocks and 20 percent in cash (including your three months of emergency living expenses).

- 30s: You want to be a tad more cautious. Roughly 70 percent of your savings should be in stocks, 10 percent should be in bonds, and 20 percent in cash (including your three months of emergency living expenses).

- 40s: You want to be even more cautious. Roughly 60 percent of your savings should be in stocks, 20 percent should be in bonds, and 20 percent in cash (including your three months of emergency living expenses).

- 50s: You want to start being careful. Roughly 50 percent of your savings should be in stocks, 30 percent should be in bonds, and 20 percent in cash (including your three months of emergency living expenses).

- 60s: You want to concentrate on preserving what you have earned. Roughly 40 percent of your savings should be in stocks, 40 percent should be in bonds, and 20 percent in cash (including your three months of emergency living expenses).

- 70s or over: You really want to keep what you have earned. Roughly 10 percent of your savings should be in stocks, 50 percent should be in bonds, and 40 percent in cash (including your three months of emergency living expenses).

How much of what you have should you invest? That, too, depends. I know you would like to be given some hard-and-fast rules, but just as the rule, "You shouldn't wear white after Labor Day" is not really a rule—and what exactly is cream if not winter white—there is no one rule for investing either.

Ideally, you should save 10 percent of your pre-tax (before taxes are taken out) money and put it into a savings account. Once you have saved your three months of living expenses, you can start to think about investing. Wait until you have around 2,500 additional dollars saved before you invest in anything other than a bank CD. While you are saving your 2,500 dollars, start to research what kinds of investments interest you. All brokers give you the option of setting up automatic monthly withdrawals from your bank accounts that will transfer an amount you specify each month from your savings or checking account to your brokerage account. As I have said elsewhere, this can be an easy way to start building up your savings. Since you won't notice the money missing each month, since you never saw it, saving becomes relatively painless. You can even set things up so your savings are automatically invested in your favorite mutual or index fund.

Once you have talked to professionals, found a broker, and have done your homework, figure out where you would like to begin to invest your money, and then buy some mutual funds or index funds (I left out individual stocks and bonds on purpose. Remember, they are not a good place for the beginning investor.)

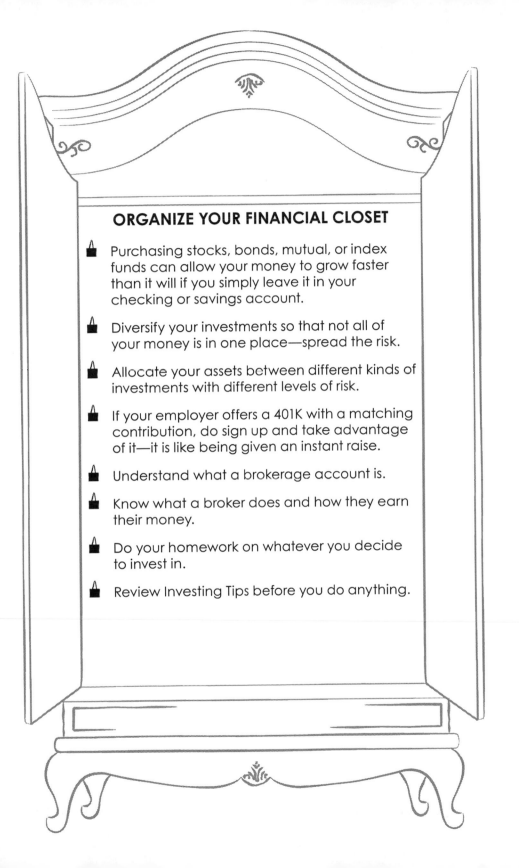

ORGANIZE YOUR FINANCIAL CLOSET

- Purchasing stocks, bonds, mutual, or index funds can allow your money to grow faster than it will if you simply leave it in your checking or savings account.

- Diversify your investments so that not all of your money is in one place—spread the risk.

- Allocate your assets between different kinds of investments with different levels of risk.

- If your employer offers a 401K with a matching contribution, do sign up and take advantage of it—it is like being given an instant raise.

- Understand what a brokerage account is.

- Know what a broker does and how they earn their money.

- Do your homework on whatever you decide to invest in.

- Review Investing Tips before you do anything.

Investing tips

If you have decided to jump in and try investing, here are some fast and easy tips to help you:

- Index funds are like the friend you borrowed the cappuccino from. Low cost, they're a good place for the new investor to begin.
- When you are young, invest in stocks—not individual stocks, but stocks in a mutual fund or index fund; save bonds for when you are older. Bonds are for playing it safe, and when you're young, you can afford to take a little more risk. Keep remembering that while riskier investments can generate more money, you can also lose more money with them, too. Still, taking some risk when you're young enough to earn it back is okay.
- If your job offers a 401K, take advantage of it. Taking money out of your paycheck before you even notice it's gone helps force you to save. And if they offer an incentive (called a matching contribution) sign up immediately.
- Get professional help—red carpet walkers know that stylists exist for a reason.
- Don't try to pick individual stocks unless you really know what you are doing (see the stylist

comment above). Even if the cute guy at the bar last night told you he was sure a certain stock is a good bet, it probably isn't, and you might keep in mind that it probably wasn't the only thing he told you that wasn't completely true.

- Avoid brokers who want to charge you high fees for every transaction.
- If you don't understand how something works, don't buy it until you do.
- There is no such thing as "get rich quick"— as always, if it sounds too good to be true, it is.
- Past performance does not guarantee future success—just because a stock has gone up in the past does not mean it will continue to do so in the future.

Investing is for the long term. Day to day, stocks and stock markets, mutual and index funds will all go up and down, and sometimes they go up and down a lot. If you did your homework before investing and kept current on your investments, you shouldn't get overly excited either way. When you invest, you are investing in your future. Pick investments with an eye for whether the company will be doing well in the future, not just today (hello, black cashmere turtleneck, goodbye, shoulder pads).

And remember, over time you can expect to earn more money by taking some considered risks than if you don't take any risks at all.

Remember, "Fashions fade, style is eternal." Yves Saint Laurent

. . .

Chapter 12: Net Worth
YOU ARE PRICELESS
(BUT CAN YOU AFFORD THE REAL THING?)

You may be priceless, but what are you worth? And by that, I mean what is your **net worth**? Net worth is a snapshot of your overall financial health, measured by adding up the total value of your assets after subtracting your liabilities.

Put simply, an **asset** is anything you own that has commercial value. Think of an asset this way: Can you sell whatever it is on eBay? Obviously, some things you own have more value than others. For example, if you own a vintage Burberry trench coat, it has a lot more value than a pair of Seven for All Mankind blue jeans. Real jewelry is worth more than fake.

So your assets include things like how much money you have—regardless of whether it's in cash, a checking account, a savings account, a money market, a CD, a stock, bond, mutual or index fund, or 401K, your clothes, your furniture, your car, or your house. If you own something and you can sell it for money, it is an asset.

On the other hand, a **liability** is an obligation; something you owe. Examples of liabilities include credit card debt, student loans, car payments, and rent or mortgage payments, or any other kind of loan.

So, again, net worth equals the total of all of your assets minus the total of all of your liabilities.

Why is it important to know your net worth? The first reason is that net worth tells you how you are doing financially overall. The second reason is that calculating your net worth on a regular basis forces you to check on your accounts—all of them. As you now know, it's important to check your accounts regularly so you know what activity is taking place in all of them. The third reason is that knowing your net worth can in itself be a motivator. If your net worth is low, there are things you can do to improve it. If it is high, continuing to improve it can help you achieve your dreams.

To calculate your net worth you need to collect information on all your assets. For example, you need to find out your account balances and the current resale value of your car. You need to find out the current value of your liabilities—for example, the amount you owe on your student debt or car loan. While it can be time-consuming to collect the information, once you have it the rest is easy. Here is an example:

	MONTH 1	MONTH 2
Assets		
Checking account	$ 1,000	$ 500
Savings account	$ 5,000	$ 5,000
Car	$ 20,00	$ 20,000
401K	$ 3,200	$ 3,500
Sub-total	$ 29,200	$ 29,000
Liabilities		
Car payment	$ 18,000	$ 17,500
Student loans	$ 20,000	$ 20,000
Credit cards	$ 250	$ -
Sub-total	$ 38,250	$ 37,500
New Worth	$ -9,050	$ -8,500
Increase or Decrease		$ 550

When you calculate your net worth, the answer by itself is not critical. What are important are the changes. If your net worth has increased from the last time you checked it, it means you have more assets and/or fewer liabilities than you did before, which is a good thing. The converse is also true—and a bad thing. The question you are answering by checking for changes in your net worth is: Am I making progress on my financial goals?

Please notice a couple of things in the example. First, total net worth is negative. I did this on purpose. If yours is too, don't panic. When you are young and starting out, your net worth is often negative. You tend to have a lot of expensive debt (student and car loans) and not a lot of assets with which to pay them off. Plus, remember from Chapter Nine, not all debt is bad, especially student debt—a college education is never, ever a waste.

If you are young, a negative net worth generally means you have not earned enough money to pay off all of your debts. As you continue to earn more money, and to save and pay off your debts, your net worth will increase. That's why your parents probably have more money than you do. If you are older, and your net worth is negative but you have a mortgage or other loans, that's okay too. The idea is to change it over time so it remains positive, with your assets exceeding your liabilities.

Second, in our example, net worth changed by a positive 550 dollars (i.e., it increased by 550 dollars). Remember, a positive change in your net worth is a good thing. Liabilities decreased by 750 dollars, the credit card balance went down 250 dollars, and the car loan went down 500 dollars. Assets decreased by 200 dollars, there was 500 dollars less in the checking account but 300 dollars more in the 401K. So, in our example, net worth became less negative. Instead of being negative 9,050 dollars, it changed to negative 8,500 dollars, a positive change of 550 dollars. Thus, to increase your net worth, you need either to increase your savings and/or decrease your debts.

Third, in our example I did not include vintage clothes or any other clothes, for that matter. Generally, other than checking and savings accounts, net worth calculations do not include assets less valuable than a car, mostly because the total value of smaller assets is not all that high. But if you have a ton of diamonds, they are, after all, a girl's best friend or, if like Carrie, you have a Manolo Blahnik shoe collection that includes future vintage classics, by all means add them in.

The saying "diamonds are a girl's best friend" was introduced in the 1949 Broadway production *Gentlemen Prefer Blondes*, in a song written by Jule Styne and Leo Robin. The musical was based on a novel by Anita Loos. It was made even more famous by Marilyn Monroe and Jane Russell in the 1953 film.

∾FASHIONISTA FACT∾

Are diamonds, in fact, always a girl's best friend? *When in doubt—fake it*! Good faux diamonds include mossanite, which costs one-tenth of real diamonds, thereby saving you a ton of money. Also, Neiman Marcus carries an excellent line of cubic zirconia faux diamonds called Fantasia.

There are net worth calculators available on the web. Google "calculate net worth" for more examples on how to calculate your net worth and for automatic net worth calculators that let you enter your information and then do the math for you.

There are two more concepts you need to learn about: Depreciation and appreciation. **Depreciation** is the loss in value of something over time. For example, every month you own a car, its value goes down a little bit; it has more miles on it, you get a door ding, it's simply been longer since it was new. **Appreciation** is just the opposite. Appreciation is the increase in value of something over time. For example, stock prices, housing prices, and fine art prices often rise over time.

Why am I telling you about appreciation and depreciation? Because, technically, when you calculate your net worth, you need to factor in how your assets have increased or decreased in value since you bought them. You do not need to adjust every single month. Simply remember, your car in year three is worth less than it was in year one, and your house is probably worth more – but very well could be worth less.

If you want to improve your net worth via shopping, the familiar rules apply: Debt is never stylish. You can mix high- and low-priced items and still achieve fashion heights. Splurge only on the classics, go downscale on the trends. Only buy what you need, and think twice about buying what you want.

• • •

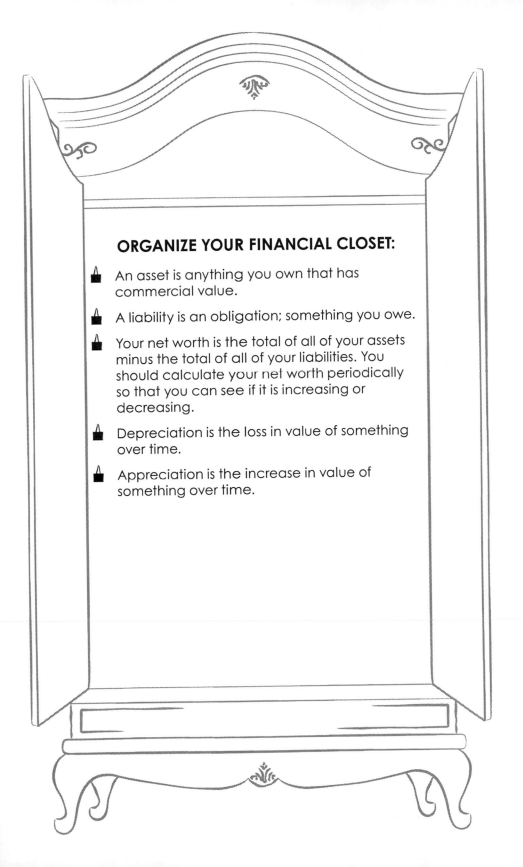

ORGANIZE YOUR FINANCIAL CLOSET:

- An asset is anything you own that has commercial value.

- A liability is an obligation; something you owe.

- Your net worth is the total of all of your assets minus the total of all of your liabilities. You should calculate your net worth periodically so that you can see if it is increasing or decreasing.

- Depreciation is the loss in value of something over time.

- Appreciation is the increase in value of something over time.

Find your financial fortune

Numerology uses the power of numbers to predict significant life cycles.

NOTE: If you take this section at all seriously, I have failed you and you should go back and re-read this entire book from cover to cover.

∽FASHIONISTA FACT∽

Per Elle Magazine, numerology was as important to Coco Chanel as white pearls and camellias. In fact, in 1921, when she decided to launch her first fragrance, Chanel No. 5, she chose the name for its numerological significance: The scent was the fifth one presented to the designer right before she was to show her fall collection on the fifth day of May.

To determine your personal number and financial fortune, begin by adding the day and month of your birth date. Continue adding until you get a single digit. For example, if your birthday is September 13, your personal number would be calculated by adding 9 + 13 = 22. Because 22 isn't a single digit you continue by adding 2 + 2 = 4. Here's what your personal number means:

Number 1:

You are a leader, impervious to pressure, and cool under fire. Budgets? No problem. Brokerage account? Got it. Savings? Absolutely. Set your goals, make those numbers do what you want, and invest in a pair of black pumps.

Number 2:

You constantly strive for balance. Zen out over numbers, meditate on environmentally correct stocks, make peace with what you have and what you don't—who needs to keep up anyway? And because of your attitude, watch your finances soar.

Number 3:

You are sociable, friendly, and outgoing. Have your friends over for a budget party. Ask the cute stockbroker to tell you all about stocks. Pursue your request for information over dinner. Wind up wealthy and attached.

Number 4:

You are a worker bee. You are practical and love details. Quick! Switch to a math, accounting, finance, economics, or business major—the rest of us need more of you. Pour over your finances, develop a sound plan, and work hard to achieve it. You will accomplish all of your goals.

Number 5:

You are a creative visionary. Color-code your budget. Add doodles and stickers and study the fantastic patterns in stock charts. Use visualization to see your future and then employ your creativity to make it happen.

Number 6:

You are loving and stable. Early on, form a plan you're comfortable after setting. Set a life goal. Stick with it and all will be well.

Number 7:

You are a deep thinker. Unfortunately, merely staring at the numbers won't change them. So get out a pencil, put those deep thoughts to work forming an actual plan, and ponder your growing fortune.

Number 8:

You are a born manager so do what you do best and manage your money. Prosperity and Prada will follow.

Number 9:

You are a teacher—study, learn, flourish, educate, and do your homework. Learn as much as you can, educate yourself, and when you invest in a fabulous tote bag, make sure it's large enough to carry your laptop.

Chapter 13: Big-ticket Items
MARC JACOBS, PRADA, DOLCE & GABBANA, AND GUCCI (KNOW YOUR DESIGNERS)

Shopping for big-ticket items is no different from shopping for smaller ones, except for the stress you put yourself under while worrying that you are about to make a huge mistake. Just think of big-ticket items as ultimate shopping.

Seriously, there are a lot of big things you will want to buy—a car, a house, an education, designer clothes, certain shoes and bags—which are big investments and will require either a lot of money and/or a lot of debt. Don't be intimidated. Making the right decision involves four things, plus courage:

- As always, weighing your wants versus your needs: You want Louis Vuitton, you need a purse
- Doing your homework
- Timing your purchase well: Big-ticket items go on sale, too
- Determining your financing: How you pay will have a big effect on the total price

Before you invest your hard-earned money on anything expensive, you need to know why you want it, if it is the right thing for you, and if there is a more affordable, satisfying substitute. You also need to think about opportunity cost: If you buy a Chanel bag that doesn't work out for you, it will set you back for a while but if you choose the wrong car, you're stuck for years.

If you can afford both the bag and the car, great, as long as you make the right selection in each case. However, if you can't afford both and really need a car, then buying a Chanel bag will, at best, slow you down and, at worst, possibly even prevent you from getting one at all.

> Buying the Chanel bag will give you less for a down payment on a car and credit card debt you should pay off first or, if you don't, a harder time making your monthly payments. The bag could even prevent you from getting the car if your liabilities become too high and your credit score goes down so much that you can't get a loan.

Although you don't want to believe it, there are other bags that probably could do the trick and that wouldn't be as likely to get in the way of your down payment on a car. Likewise, you need to really think about what kind of car you want in terms of what you can afford. Yes, you would look smashing in that little red convertible I keep mentioning. I don't doubt it for a second. However, down the line you might look, or at least feel, even better in a more sensible hybrid.

Also, before buying a big-ticket item, make sure you've figured in what all the extra costs will be. For example, little red convertibles use more gas and have higher insurance rates than most other types of cars, and the newer the car, the higher the annual registration fee in many states. Big houses come with more property taxes, higher heating and air conditioning bills, and require more upkeep costs than smaller houses. Occasionally—rarely, but occasionally—Ben & Jerry's can succeed in diverting me, at least temporarily, from my shoe problem. However, in so doing, Ben & Jerry's adds to my thigh problem, yet another example of how every action has its consequences.

Before taking the plunge, you must do research on your purchase. Sticking with our car example for a moment, there are a lot of questions you must think about and need answers to before you buy. You've checked your budget and know how much you can afford to spend. Now there are other decisions you need to make. New or used? Gas intensive or hybrid? Four-door, two-door, or SUV? How long do you plan to keep the car? What makes are you interested in? Colors? Extras? Which dealer in your area has the cheapest price? The list goes on, but you get the idea. You should ask these kinds of questions about every big-ticket item you buy. Unless he was determined to surprise you, you wouldn't let your significant other buy you diamonds without knowing all about the four C's, would you?

As always, do your homework wherever and however you can—by researching on the Internet or at the library, asking your friends and family, and by talking to professionals.

Third, you need to time your purchase correctly, both in terms of your own finances and situation and in terms of getting the best deal. Some big-ticket items regularly go on sale at certain times during the year. Be patient and wait for those times. Sometimes patience is a virtue. Car dealers offer lower process from July to October and even more during the last two weeks of December. Winter can be the best time to buy a house, since houses tend to show better with foliage, green grass, and flowers to enhance their curb appeal. Avoid big gift-giving holidays when buying jewelry, especially Valentine's Day. Traveling and weddings also have off-seasons. The cost of not waiting can be high. For example, 10 percent off a twenty-thousand dollar car is two thousand dollars. Think of all the things you could buy with two thousand dollars. Is it really worth two thousand dollars to you to have the car a few months earlier? I would think not. It's true that sometimes you can't wait to time your purchase. But if you can, you can definitely save money by knowing the right time to buy. So, just say no to impulse purchases—especially big ones!

Finally, the more of your own money you use pay for what you buy, the less money you will have to borrow and pay interest on, so the cheaper the money you borrow will be. For example, when you buy a home, lenders require you pay a certain amount up front—a down payment—and the amount they require is often expressed as a percent of the total price. The higher your down payment, the lower your interest rate may be, and, in addition, your credit score could even improve. This is true for any big purchase. You need to save as much money as you can before purchasing, so you can borrow less money to get it. While saving up for a down payment, you can also research and take time deciding exactly what to buy and what the opportunity costs of your choice may be.

By following these four steps—sorting your wants versus your needs, doing your homework, timing your purchases correctly, and determining your financing needs—you will help turn a daunting purchase decision into a much easier one. Even so, you can expect to have buyer's remorse. It happens all the time. You knew exactly what you wanted and now that you have it, you're kicking yourself for not having gotten it in a different color, or a larger or smaller size, or you paid too much, or … you get the point. So be prepared. Keep remembering that it's all just shopping.

In the next section, there are tips on how to buy designer clothes, cars, and houses and how to rent an apartment. Keep in mind that these suggestions are bare-bones. They merely provide a foundation on which to build, like a black camisole and tights, but it's a necessary foundation if you want to go out in the world feeling well-dressed.

How to buy designer clothes

We love our designers. We love their originality, expert tailoring and fit, their sumptuous fabrics, and most of all their style. But, when—notice I did not say if—you buy designer clothes, there are some specific things you should look for. These suggestions, from *InStyle Secrets of Style*, will also help you tell real from fake. While there are many designers we trust, price is not always an indicator of quality, and there are unscrupulous counterfeiters who want to sell a fake as real. If you are going to spend this kind of money (when and how did two hundred dollar-plus jeans become *de rigueur?*) you need to look at:

De rigueur is a French expression literally meaning "of rigor" or "of strictness." In English language usage, it means, "necessary according to etiquette, protocol, or fashion." But it sounds so much better in French, doesn't it?

- Fabric: When you buy expensive items, shop with your hands. Fabrics should feel wonderful (the technical term) to the touch.
- Hems: Should be double-stitched and invisible on the outside of the garment.
- Seams: Should run straight, with no puckers.
- Stitching: Should be secure and straight (with eight to twelve stitches per inch), and all of the excess stitching should be cut away.
- Lining: Should be made of soft fabric; if it is stiff it will ruin the drape.
- Buttons: Should match, meet the buttonhole perfectly, be secure, and if the fabric is heavy, should be attached with fabric or plastic disks on the inside.
- Zippers: Should be hidden and dyed to match the garment (unless they are supposed to stand out—think Dolce & Gabbana).
- Patterns: Should match on all seams. If it is a dress, the patterns should match at the top and the bottom.

"Never confuse elegance with snobbery." Yves Saint Laurent

Buying classic designer pieces is great and sensible only if the fit is incredible, the piece is original in design, it's a great basic you'll wear over and over again, and you simply love it because of how it totally expresses your personality. If it is a trendy style, don't do it! Get the knock-off at GUESS, Zara, H&M, Bebe, and ABS. Those stores are expert at copying / "interpreting" designer looks and retailing them for a fraction of the price. When to scrimp, when to splurge? Splurge on classic timeless pieces like those great-fitting pants and that perfectly cut black jacket. Since they look terrific on you, you'll wear them everywhere. Scrimp on trendy items so that six months later you'll be able to afford the next new style that comes along.

When is it a good time to start buying designer? If you're young and all about the three-month trend, you should probably wait until you're ready to have more long-term items in your wardrobe. Even if your finances are under control, it's not a good idea to buy designer if what you've bought will be "out" in a few months. If you are older, thinking about investing in classics and can afford the price, go ahead and get started.

Also, a good Fashionista should keep in mind her birthday, holidays, and other gift-giving occasions. If you love a designer piece and simply must have it—enter friends and family. Your loved ones never know what to get you, so why not be subtly suggestive and end up with what you really want, without straining your wardrobe budget? Now you're smart-shopping.

How to buy a car

You've decided to buy a car. You have followed the earlier instructions from this chapter and have sorted your wants versus your needs. You've done your homework (*Edmunds, How Stuff Works,* and *Kelly Blue Book* all have good websites and much of this information comes from them), timed your purchase (unless it was impossible to do so), and determined how you are going to pay for it. What else should you know?

1. Buy used (but not too used). A new car loses 10 percent of its value the minute you drive it off the lot. Let someone else over-pay for those first few miles of breaking the car in.

2. Know your budget. I said it before and I'll say it again: You must know what you're committing to in terms of what you can afford. Buying a car involves much more than its initial purchase price. It also requires gas, insurance, taxes, registration fees, and maintenance, never mind the service costs. *Consumer Reports* (www.consumerreports.org) has a website that is helpful.

3. Know what your old car is worth before you go to a car dealer to buy a new one, and certainly before you make a private party sale. *Kelly Blue Book* is a great website for this (www.kbb.com).

4. Know what other car you would be willing to buy if you can't get the specific one you want. You must

give yourself more than one option so that you are less likely to let yourself get talked into a bad deal by a good salesperson.

5. Know how the car you want drives. Go for a test drive, but agree with yourself before you step foot on a car lot that you will not buy the car that day, no matter what. If a friend or family member has the car you want, drive theirs. The longer you stay off the car lot between the day you test drive and the day you purchase, the better position you will put yourself in when it is time to buy. You need distance from the shiny new object of your affection in order to be able to negotiate effectively for it.

6. Understand what incentives the dealer is offering. All of them. An incentive is the items they say they "throw in" if you buy now, today. The longer you hold out, the more they will throw your way. Don't agree to buy until they quit giving you things. Then, check out the dealer's website to see if there are incentives such as a contents or rebates that your salesperson neglected to mention. It happens. Sometimes. Make sure you understand the total value of what they have offered you.

7. Negotiate each piece of the deal separately. First negotiate what you are going to pay for the new car. That way you have a starting number you have agreed on. Then, if you are doing a trade-in, negotiate the value of your old car. Once you

have agreed on that price, subtract the new car price from the old car price and arrange financing for a sale or terms for a lease.

8. If leasing instead of buying, be sure you understand the terms. Thoroughly. What's the interest rate being used to figure the lease payments? What do you pay if you drive extra miles? What's the down payment? What are the penalties for late payments?

9. Know what your loan will cost. Use a car loan calculator (there are plenty on the Internet) to figure this out. (Google "car loan calculator.")

10. Negotiate who will pay the extra costs. Either you or the dealer has to pay for taxes on the purchase, registration fees, and other costs. So be sure the price you've negotiated is the "out the door" price that includes these costs.

11. Last, but not least, bring a book or something to do. It may sound silly, but car dealers are notorious for letting you sit there in the hope you will get bored enough to agree to a higher price. Don't let them.

How to rent an apartment

Many of these tips came from howstuffworks.com which also has other advice for first time apartment renters. There also websites which offer advice on finding and interviewing roommates.

1. Know how much rent you can afford. How do you know? Your budget, of course.
2. Choose a neighborhood you want to live in.
3. Look for an apartment in newspapers, online, on school and community bulletin boards, and by asking around.
4. Look for services to help you find a roommate if you cannot afford your own apartment and will need to share (some of these charge fees). You can also look on websites such as *Craig's List* (www.craig-slist.com).
5. Prepare your personal information. Landlords will want to know about your previous rental history, your earnings, your credit report, and your personal references.
6. When you go to see an apartment, look at the whole building, not just the apartment itself. Is there any damage you can see (like water stains or cracks)? Are the common areas nicely kept? What about the washer and dryer? What is the parking situation? What amenities does the building offer (Pool? Cable? Satellite? Gym? Are pets allowed?)? If you see any occupants, ask them questions—it is amazing what people will tell you.
7. Negotiate the rent, if possible. In a high-demand area, around colleges for example, the rent is what it is. However, in many areas you can negoti-

ate. If you don't feel comfortable doing it, bring someone with you to help, or for moral support.

8. Read the lease. All of it. Every word. Be sure you know what you are agreeing to be responsible for, when the rent is due, what you can and cannot do. Find out how much of a security deposit they want (landlords ask for money up front in case of damages, then return the money to you when you move out, subtracting whatever it costs them to repair any damage you may have done). Also, be sure to find out what happens at the end of the lease—can you automatically renew or can they kick you out just when you are getting comfortable?

9. Spend some time in the space, if you can. Make sure it feels good to you before you sign. Ideally, visit the building, if not the apartment, at different times of day or on a weekday in addition to a weekend. You may see the apartment in an entirely different light.

How to buy a house

You've decided to leave the world of renting and take the plunge into home ownership. Be sure you have thought through your options very carefully. Why are you buying? Why now? Because home prices are low and interest rates are favorable so it's a good investment? Or are you facing a life change and just need more room? Can you afford the upkeep?

A good rule of thumb for how much home you can afford: Add up what your mortgage will be, plus your property taxes, plus your insurance. The total should not exceed 33 percent of your gross salary. If you pay more than that, your mortgage will be so high that your other bills can quickly become too high, and if there is some kind of emergency, you might not be able to cover your payments.

Ideally, you should have enough money saved up to enable you to pay 20 percent of the purchase price as a down payment. Remember, the more money you pay up front, the less money you need to borrow to purchase the house, so the less total interest you will pay, meaning that you will spend less on the house in total. Also remember that the less money you borrow, the lower your interest rate may be and your credit score could improve.

Here are some of the main steps to take in buying a house from *The Savvy Woman's Home Buying Handbook* by Tara-Nicholle Nelson:

1. Get educated about the buying and financing process
2. Hire a Realtor. A realtor is a licensed professional who helps you find and navigate the home-buying process. Almost always, the seller pays the cost of the realtor, so find one you like and get started looking.

3. Get pre-approval for your mortgage. This way, sellers will know you are a "real/serious" buyer and will be willing to accept your offer and to negotiate.

4. House-hunt. The steps are very similar to renting an apartment: Find the right neighborhoods, look at a variety of houses in the price range you can afford, pick one you like, talk to the neighbors, and spend time in the space.

5. Once you've decided on a home, write an offer. Your realtor will help you with all this.

6. Have your realtor present your offer and work with you to negotiate the purchase price and contract.

7. Open escrow. You will be asked to write an "earnest" check, which is often three percent of the purchase price, so be ready.

8. Conduct inspections—you will want to hire a professional to check out the roof, electrical system, plumbing, structural integrity, whether there are termites, etc.

9. Select homeowner's insurance and a home warranty. Mortgage companies require you to purchase insurance, to cover your new home and property, as well as to protect yourself.

10. Pay your down payment and finalize your mortgage arrangements.

11. Sign documents and close the deal.

12. Move in! Be sure to buy yourself some flowers and a bottle of champagne, if no one else does it for you.

I gave one of the biggest purchases you'll ever make the briefest list—just to give you an idea of what's involved. Enough to know that there is a lot of homework and research to do.

• • •

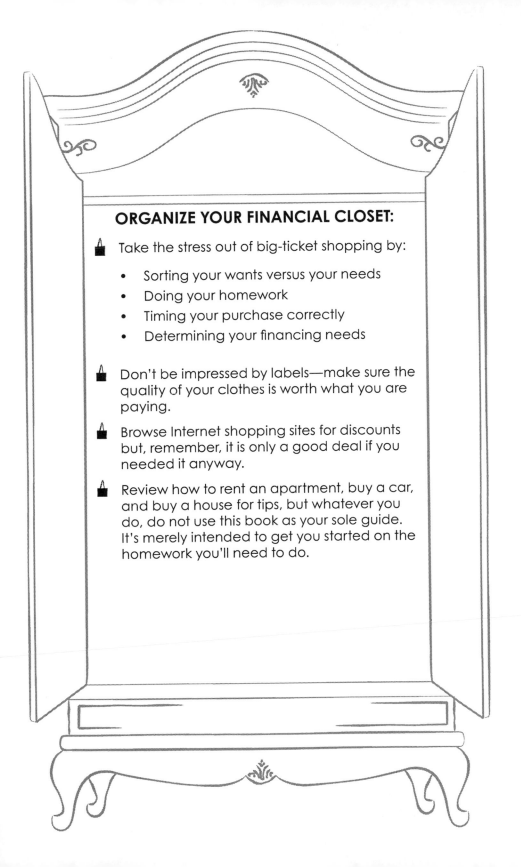

ORGANIZE YOUR FINANCIAL CLOSET:

- Take the stress out of big-ticket shopping by:

    - Sorting your wants versus your needs
    - Doing your homework
    - Timing your purchase correctly
    - Determining your financing needs

- Don't be impressed by labels—make sure the quality of your clothes is worth what you are paying.

- Browse Internet shopping sites for discounts but, remember, it is only a good deal if you needed it anyway.

- Review how to rent an apartment, buy a car, and buy a house for tips, but whatever you do, do not use this book as your sole guide. It's merely intended to get you started on the homework you'll need to do.

Chapter 14: Insurance
AVOID A BAD HAIR DAY (OR WORSE)

There's nothing worse—well, maybe not *nothing*—than spending all morning washing, blow-drying, combing and brushing, curling and straightening your hair only to have turn out looking awful. Bad hair days: We all have them and we all dread them. But you only have to think "hat," and suddenly a bad hair day turns into a good hat day! Plus you can be pretty sure that the next time you wash your hair, it will look smashing.

Unfortunately, other awful things can happen to you that can't just be washed away—things like car accidents, getting seriously sick, or losing your job. In such cases, resorting to stop gap measures or merely hoping tomorrow will be better is not a great plan. Your car will need to be fixed immediately, you will need to go to the doctor, you will need to be able to pay your rent or mortgage, and you will need to be able to pay for everything while still being able to afford food and everyday expenses, preferably without asking for a bailout from your folks or friends. How can you manage to do all this?

One way, as we've discussed, is to keep up to three months of living expenses in your savings account as a cash cushion to help tide you over when emergencies happen. And they will—they happen to everyone. Another way to handle life's problems is to buy **insurance**.

When you take out insurance, you pay a fixed amount of money to the insurance company in the event something specific goes wrong. If the bad event you've insured yourself against happens, the insurance company pays whatever they agree it costs up to a maximum—and it can amount to a lot—to help you fix the problem. The problems can range from car repairs, doctor bills, and rent to a mortgage. What they pay you for, and how much they pay you, depends upon what kind and how much insurance you buy.

How does insurance work? Say you pay a small amount every month for a few months, and then something bad happens and you need help. How can the insurance company help you and make a profit? They are able to help because lots of other people have bought insurance too, and they combine your money with the money those other people have been paying. And, fortunately, not everyone has a problem that requires an insurance pay-out at the same time. Also, fortunately, the number of people who *don't* have bad things happen is generally greater than the number of people who do. Think of insurance like a slot machine in Vegas: Lots of people put a little money in but only a few people get a lot out. There is one big difference, though: Since insurance just gets you back to zero, if you're lucky, and at best usually involves a lot of inconvenience, it is one game you don't want to hit the jackpot playing!

There are a lot of different kinds of insurance. If you are willing to pay to protect it (whatever the "it" is), there is no doubt an insurance company willing to cover you.

> Some interesting body parts that have purportedly been insured include: David Beckham's legs and feet for 70 million, the legs of Lord of the Dance's Michael Flatley for 39 million dollars, America Ferrera's teeth for 10 million, Bruce Springsteen's voice for six million dollars, Keith Richard's middle finger for 1.6 million and Mariah Carrey's legs for one billion dollars.

Some common kinds of insurance are: Car (in case of accidents), health (in case you get sick), property (in case of theft or damage), renter's (in case of theft or damage to personal property you own, such as your furniture and valuables), disability (in case you get incapacitated), life (in case of death), and natural disasters (in case of earthquakes, floods, wildfires, etc.), So what kinds of insurance should you buy? The answer depends upon your specific situation. At a minimum, you need:

 Liability insurance on your car (which is required by law)

 Health insurance on you, and

 Property/renters insurance (for your valuables and/or house, if you have

> Before accepting a job, ask if health insurance is offered and how much you will have to pay of its cost.

one). If you rent and are affected by a fire, flood, theft, roof leakage, electrical shortage, plumbing accident, etc., renter's insurance can protect your belongings. Your landlord will have property insurance, but it will only cover the property they own, like the roof, floors, and walls. It will not cover your personal belongings.

If you can afford it, full insurance coverage on your car is best because it covers injuries to both you and your car. If you have a liability-only policy, you are protected against having to compensate other people if you hurt them or their property with your car. The policy will help pay for a lawyer to fight a lawsuit brought by the other person, for example, but injuries to you are not covered. That means you will have to have your own car repaired or pay your doctors for their services.

Once you have the basics covered, you can start to think about additional types of insurance or adding more coverage to what you already have.

➤ Disability insurance. If you become sick or injured and can't work for an extended period of time, disability insurance can help you pay your bills by replacing a portion of your income, generally between 45 percent and 60 percent, until you recover. But there are generally more reasons not to buy disability insurance than to buy it. For example, if you have a spouse or significant other who can cover your expenses, or enough savings to see you through for a while, or if your credit is good enough for you to borrow the money you need, then it is probably not worth paying for since the odds of your becoming disabled are, frankly, pretty low. On the other hand, if you are your sole source of income, you should think about getting it, but, as always, do your homework first.

- Life insurance. Life insurance pays an amount of money to whomever you designate if you, well, die. If you have children or are the primary wage earner for your family, you should have life insurance. Your untimely death will disrupt your loved ones' lives and they will probably need to have extra money to tide them over with big expenses like mortgage payments until things settle down. If you are single, childless, and are not the family's sole support, then you don't need it.

- Natural disaster insurance. Natural disasters do happen and if you own your own house or property, are somewhere where a disaster is likely to occur (like California with its earthquakes or the Gulf Coast with its floods and hurricanes), and can afford it, it is a good idea to have it. The premium will be expensive, but it should be measured against the potential cost of the disaster happening to you. There are a few places where natural disaster insurance is mandatory. For example in designated flood areas. You need to check to see if this is the case in your area.

The best insurance polices are not always the most expensive. Rather, the best policy is the one that fits you best, at a price you can afford. How do you find the best policy for you? Through an **insurance broker**. Like many salespeople, they are paid on commission, but by the insurance company, not you, so don't hesitate to call one to ask for help.

Rates vary by company and are based on a variety of factors. For example, health insurance rates depend on your age and previous illnesses; car insurance rates depend on your driving record, age, and the type of car you drive. When you buy insurance can be a factor in determining how much you pay for it. If you buy earthquake insurance right after an earthquake has occurred, it will cost you more than it would have right before, or several years later. Various discounts are offered, such as lower car insurance rates for good drivers and good students. Insurance companies will frequently lower your rates if you have more than one policy with them.

Before you call a broker, there are some terms (insurance language) the broker will use and you should know before you start shopping. (Yes, this too is shopping. Really, what isn't?)

- **Policy** is what you buy when you pay for insurance—for example, a car insurance policy or a medical insurance policy.

- **Premium** is the amount of money you pay for the policy.
- **Risk** is the chance something will happen requiring the insurance company's financial assistance. Everyone's risk level is different, and insurance companies are the ones who evaluate it. For example, someone who has a drunk-driving record will pay more for car insurance than someone whose driving record is clean because the risk of the driver who drinks having an accident is much higher.
- **Loss** is what is caused by the occurrence of a bad event. It is paid for by the insurance company.
- **Claim** is what you tell the insurance company you need. (Your phone call to them constitutes a claim.) You can also ask your insurance broker to file a claim for you.
- **Proof of loss** is what you give to the insurance company when they ask you to prove what costs you need to be reimbursed for. Insurance companies won't just take your word for it that you need money. They are going to want to see the wrecked car or the itemized bill from your doctor. Keep all your receipts to give to them.
- **Deductible** is the portion of the insured claim that you pay for (i.e., the portion the

insurance company is not responsible for). When you purchase an insurance policy, you agree to pay the initial amount of money that is needed to pay for whatever damages occurred. The insurance policy will then cover the rest. For example, if you purchase a health insurance policy with a five hundred dollar deductible, you are responsible for the first five hundred dollars in medical bills you incur each year. The higher your deductible (the more you agree to pay), the less the policy will cost you). Why? Because the cost of some claims won't exceed the deductible, something the insurance company calculates in determining how much they are going to charge you.

🥿 **Liability** is the legal term for what your responsibility is to other people. For example, if you are in a car accident that is your fault, you have a responsibility to help any victims of the accident get their car repaired and to pay for their medical injuries. You have a "liability" to them.

Wouldn't it be great if there was bad hair day insurance? That way, if you had a bad hair day, you could call the insurance company, get some money for the disaster that has befallen you, and go to a salon.

How to choose an insurance broker

Once you have decided you need insurance, you need to find an insurance company by checking with your friends, family, and other references such as the Internet. You want a company with good customer service, who will be on your side when you have a claim instead of opposing you, and will assign you a broker you like and trust. You also want to know if the company is financially sound. Fortunately, insurance companies are graded on their ability to pay claims and on how well they manage their money. You can Google "insurance company report cards" to see the status of a company you're considering doing business with. The insurance company's score should not be the only thing you look at, but if it has a low score, you should think hard before signing on with them.

Every state has a department called Consumer Affairs, a great place to call and ask about insurance companies. While they won't tell you what company to choose, they will give you some guidelines about which companies have good reputations in your state by providing you with complaint records, financial score information, and company phone numbers so you can call them. Finally, find out which companies will offer you a discount. Like good sales, discounts can save you money.

Besides checking on discounts, there are other things you can do to keep premiums low. As we've seen, insurance companies base the rate they charge for car insurance on your age, gender, the type of car you drive, your credit score (another reason to care about credit scores), and your driving record (whether you have had a lot of tickets or accidents). While you can't do anything about your gender or your age, you can: Avoid getting speeding tickets, drive safely, try to qualify for every type of discount you can (a good academic record does matter), pick your car wisely (that nifty little sports car will cost more to insure than a sensible white four-door—even though it is more fun). Also, many insurance companies offer quotes online. You can check out and compare policies pretty easily on the Internet.

Insurance companies are rated on (among other things) their size and strength, because both affect their ability to pay claims. In insurance, size really does matter, and bigger is often better.

• • •

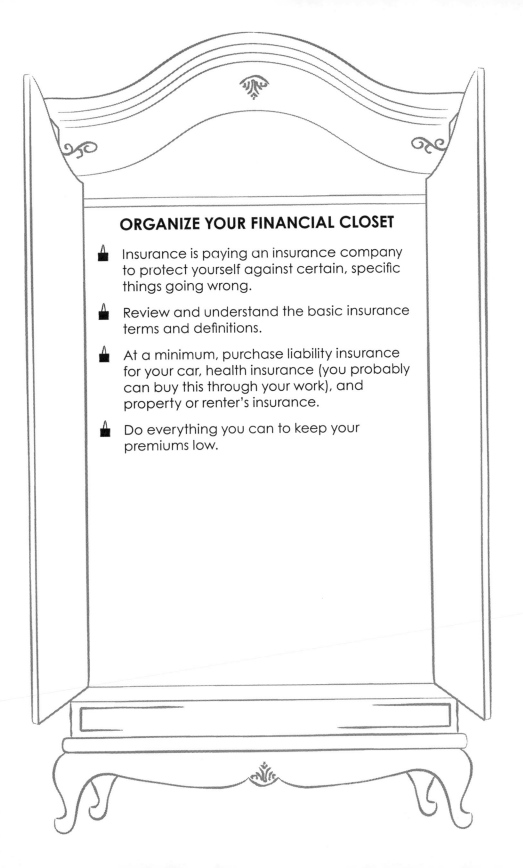

ORGANIZE YOUR FINANCIAL CLOSET

- Insurance is paying an insurance company to protect yourself against certain, specific things going wrong.

- Review and understand the basic insurance terms and definitions.

- At a minimum, purchase liability insurance for your car, health insurance (you probably can buy this through your work), and property or renter's insurance.

- Do everything you can to keep your premiums low.

Chapter 15: Taxes

FACE THE FACTS (LIKE AGING, THEY'RE INEVITABLE)

You're young. You don't have wrinkles yet...but you will. Don't worry. Although getting old is inevitable, it's better than the alternative, and *looking* old is *not* inevitable. Modern medicine is here to help you out along with cosmetic companies, dermatologists, and plastic surgeons. You can buy a new and improved you. So now, only death, taxes, and the certain knowledge that black is slimming remain constants.

So wrinkles, you can avoid; taxes, you can't. But unlike wrinkles, taxes can help you feel good about yourself. How? Because the more taxes you have to pay, the more money you have earned. On the plus side, the pain of paying taxes is less than the pain or price tag from fixing wrinkles. I don't care what they say, needles hurt.

> ### ∾ FASHIONISTA FACT: ∾
> Nowadays, teenagers(!) are starting the quest for eternal youth before they even enter college. A growing number of them are buying into Botox even before they graduate from high school. All I can say is, stop it! There is plenty of time to freeze your face. At upwards of three hundred dollars per appointment, it is a waste of your money. Instead, pay off your credit card debt and save or invest your money.

But what exactly are taxes? Taxes are fees people must pay to help support federal, state, and local governments. They are used to fund public schools and community colleges and universities; they pay for police, fire departments, and the military; they pay for roads, and provide a host of community services. No one likes paying them, but they are part of the cost of living in a modern civilized society. If you don't like what the government is spending your money on, you have to vote into office people who you think will make better decisions.

There are a lot of different kinds of taxes. There are **income taxes,** which are taxes you pay based on—you guessed it—your income. You pay a portion of whatever money you earn to the government. There are **investment taxes,** which are taxes you pay based on—you guessed it again—your investments (these are technically called **capital gains taxes).** There are **sales taxes,** which are taxes on the things you buy. There are **property taxes,** which are taxes based on property. If you do not own a house, building, or land, you obviously don't have to worry about property taxes. There are **excise taxes,** which are also known as sin taxes because they tax items like liquor, cigarettes and cigars, and gambling, which some people think of as sinful. Also, the tax we pay on gasoline for our cars is considered an excise tax. And finally, lest you worry you are carrying all of these tax burdens on your shoulders alone, there are also **corporate taxes.** These are the taxes companies pay based on their profits.

Let's start with your paycheck. If you look at it closely, you will see that your **net paycheck**—the money you actually take home—is a smaller number than your **gross pay**, what you actually earned. Your employer deducts your share of income taxes out of your salary and pays it to the government on your behalf. Why do they do this? It's the law. When you start a new job, you are required to fill out a form called a **W-4** that gives your employer permission to deduct taxes from your paycheck. How do they know how much to take out? They are able to make an educated guess because they know what you earn (remember, income taxes are based on what you earn) and they have your answers to the questions on your W-4 form.

The first question on a W-4 is about your martial status. There is a different tax rate for single people than for married people. Until recently, you had to pay more taxes when you got married—one good reason to stay single. The next question is about your **withholding allowance**, a number you can choose. That number tells your employer how much or how little you will pay in taxes, based on other things happening in your life—whether you have dependent children or lots of special tax deductions, like high medical expenses and other things.

The more allowances you claim, the less income tax your employer withholds; so the fewer allowances you claim down to none, the more income tax your employer withholds. Usually, you claim one allowance apiece for yourself, your spouse, and each of your children, if you have any. However, you can adjust the number of allowances for your situation in order to avoid having too much or not enough taxes withheld. But don't get greedy. When you file your taxes in April each year, the truth will come out, and if you try to game the system, you might pay "tax penalties" on the amount the government calculates you underreported, so do the right thing.

The good news is you do not have to figure this out all on your own. You can find websites and calculators to help you determine how much withholding allowance you should take and the W-4 form itself has a worksheet you can use, although it does involve a bit of math.

> The federal government has a calculator to help you determine how much withholding allowance you should claim. You can find it at: www.irs.gov/individuals/article/id=96196,00.html

Special note: If you have more than one job, be sure you claim zero allowances at your second job. By claiming zero, the highest amount of tax will be withheld. Why do this? Because presumably you've used up all your allowances on your first job, so all your money from your second job is extra and, unfortunately, fully taxed.

So the total amount of income taxes deducted from your paycheck depends on how much you earn, where you live, your martial status, and how many withholding allowances you declare.

Now let's talk about the many and varied tax deductions that are taken from what you earn. Most of you pay five—yes, five—kinds of payroll taxes, based on your income. And if you work in some big cities, like New York, you pay even more. Taxes deducted from your paycheck are:

1. **Medicare.** Medicare taxes equal 1.45 percent of your gross earnings and are used by the federal government to aid people over sixty-five with their medical care.

2. **Social Security taxes** take 6.2 percent of your gross earnings and are used by the federal government to help people who are retired or disabled. There is a limit on this tax, which is set by the federal government and changes annually.

   The true name for Social Security is the Federal Insurance Contributions Act (FICA).

3. **Federal income taxes** take between 10 percent and 35 percent of your gross income, and the federal government uses them to pay for things like national defense and assistance to state and local governments as well as a huge number of other programs. The reason the percentage range is so large is that people who earn more money pay higher tax rates than people who earn less money. So those who earn very little money may only pay 10 percent of their

income in federal income taxes while those who have a very high income can pay as much as 35 percent of their income in federal income taxes. This is why I said earlier, the more taxes you pay, the more money you've earned.

4. **State income taxes** vary widely. In some states, it is zero percent while in others it is as high as 10 to 11 percent of your gross income. State income taxes are used to pay for state projects. There is also State Disability Insurance (SDI) and State Unemployment Insurance (SUI) in some states.

5. **Local income taxes** imposed by counties, towns, and cities also vary widely depending on where you live, and are used to pay for local projects.

One thing to note: Sometimes taxes have different names so you might need to look something up if you don't see it listed here, but all taxes fall into one of these categories.

Investment taxes (capital gain taxes) are a little different. If you invest your money and earn more than 750 dollars in one year from your investment, you pay a capital gain tax. When you sell a stock or bond for a higher price that is higher than the price at which you bought it, you will pay tax on anything over the extra money you made. So if you bought twenty shares of stock at one hundred dollars per share, then sold them for 150 dollars per share, you made one thousand dollars. That one thousand dollars difference is called a gain and you will pay tax on it. You only pay the tax when you sell. So as long as you decide to keep your stock, you won't be taxed. The amount of tax you will have to pay on capital gains depends not only upon how much money you made, but also on how long you owned the stock. Generally investments held for one year or longer are taxed at a much lower rate. So plan ahead.

The rest of the taxes listed above are either paid at the time of the transaction (sales and excise taxes) or when a bill is sent to you from the government (federal, state, and property taxes). Remember in the Terrified of Math pop quiz, when I asked if you had remembered to figure in taxes? I was referring to sales taxes. Let's re-do Question 1 from the Pop Quiz, and let's assume you live in San Francisco, California, where the sales tax rate is 9.5 percent.

You have 100 dollars. The fabulous scarf in the window, which could easily double as a belt, costs 50 dollars. Can you buy it in two colors? The answer is no, you can only buy one. Why?

- Two scarves equal 100 dollars
- Sales tax equals 9.5 percent
- One hundred dollars times 9.5 percent equals 9.50 dollars

So the total for the two scarves is 109.50 dollars and you only have 100 dollars. Very sad. But you can still buy one!

Now let's talk a little more about income taxes. When do you pay this tax? Well, as you have just seen, you pay a lot of estimated income tax during the year through your paycheck. Then every April, you have to tell the government what you've earned and calculate how much tax you owe by filing an income tax form.

How will the government know if you are telling the truth? At the end of the year, your employer gives you a form called a **W-2**. They also give the government a copy of this form. The W-2 is the employer's record of what you earned and the taxes they deducted on your behalf and paid to the government. When you send in your income tax form, you attach your W-2 to it. That way, the government can compare what you said with what your employer said. And believe me, they do compare, so don't try to cheat. If they catch you cheating, not only will you pay interest on the taxes you owe and possibly penalties, but they may well put you on a computer list as someone to check more carefully in the future, and who wants that?

What if you earned money from freelance jobs, not from a nine to five job, or from your investments? That money is also considered income and will need to be reported on your income tax form each April. On the income tax form, there is a section called **Schedule C.** That is where you include income that did not come from a full-time employer. You also report your investment profits (capital gains) in another section of the income tax form. If you are fortunate enough to earn a lot of money from investments, you may have to pay estimated taxes quarterly during the year.

Remember good debt and bad debt? The concept comes back into play when you think about taxes. Generally the interest on the good kind of debt, for example mortgage interest and some student loan interest, is tax-deductible. This means that when you file your taxes, you get to subtract some of the interest you paid from your income and only pay taxes on the net amount. There are limits. Ask an accountant or family member knowledgeable about taxes for help if you need to. Interest on bad debt—credit cards and car loans, for example—is not tax-deductible. The government does not want to reward you for incurring bad debts so you do not get to subtract any credit when you file your taxes.

If you earn enough income to reach one of the higher tax brackets, you probably need to get someone to help you calculate your income taxes, both on a **standardized deduction** and on an **itemized deduction** basis. A standard deduction is the government's estimate of the value of the average person's itemized deductions. If you don't earn much money, standard deductions work in your favor. But if you earn more, don't settle for average. Itemizing such deductions as expensive health care, charitable donations, property taxes, mortgage interest, car registration, and professional help in preparing your taxes cam reduce the taxes you pay.

There is a lot more to know about tax planning. This has just scratched the surface. So how do you figure all this out to know how much you need to pay in taxes? Some people go on the Internet or use a financial program, such as Turbo Tax, and do it themselves. Others pay a certified public accountant. A CPA can save you tax money by identifying tax loopholes and the effect of other complicated rules and regulations that you would probably overlook. Still others go to a tax preparer like H&R Block. No matter which way you decide to go, be ready to answer questions, and organize your income and expense information and bring it with you. You will, of course, have saved your receipts in order to create and stick to your budget. But if you have also been using an automated financial program, you will be doubly rewarded. These programs can be time-consuming in the beginning while you learn the program and get used to using it, but they make figuring out your taxes quick and easy and offer an added benefit of helping you know how and where you spent your money.

Regardless of which taxes you are required to pay and how much, just know that for taxes, unlike wrinkles, there is no cure.

• • •

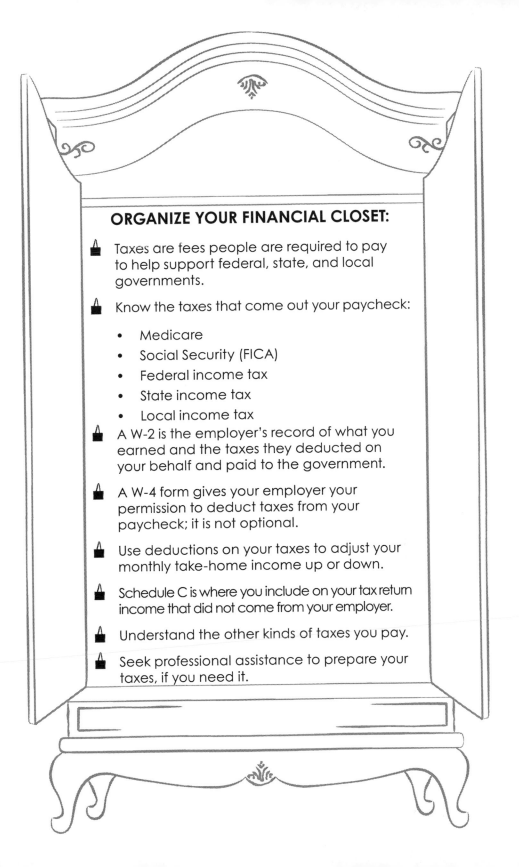

ORGANIZE YOUR FINANCIAL CLOSET:

- Taxes are fees people are required to pay to help support federal, state, and local governments.

- Know the taxes that come out your paycheck:
  - Medicare
  - Social Security (FICA)
  - Federal income tax
  - State income tax
  - Local income tax

- A W-2 is the employer's record of what you earned and the taxes they deducted on your behalf and paid to the government.

- A W-4 form gives your employer your permission to deduct taxes from your paycheck; it is not optional.

- Use deductions on your taxes to adjust your monthly take-home income up or down.

- Schedule C is where you include on your tax return income that did not come from your employer.

- Understand the other kinds of taxes you pay.

- Seek professional assistance to prepare your taxes, if you need it.

Chapter 16: Professional Help
PERSONAL STYLISTS (PREVENT A FASHION TRAIN WRECK)

It's a fine line between super stylish and fashion train wreck—especially if you don't have a stylist. A little professional help goes a long way. Is it expensive? Not necessarily, and, besides, what's a little extra cash if you can avoid appearing on the "don't" page of a magazine with a black bar across your face? Being labeled fashion road-kill is never a good thing.

The same is true for your finances. Look to experts for guidance. As we've seen, there are many available to help you get your financial closet in order, and each can help you with a specific goal or within a specific area. Let's review the possibilities:

- Accountant: An accountant, who is usually but not always a CPA, helps you maintain your financial records and prepares and submits your tax returns. You customarily pay for their services by the hour or with a flat fee. A CPA is trained to know the ins and outs of current tax laws and can find legitimate ways to help reduce what you pay. Also, the fee for their services is tax deductible.

- Attorney: Attorneys provide legal advice, set up trusts, wills, powers of attorney, and the like. They also help with pre-nuptial agreements and divorces. Attorneys are kind of like your best girlfriend; they'll tell you the unadorned truth, prepare you for the worst, and help you sue the bastard if things don't work out. Some attorneys specialize in tax law and can do many of the same things accountants can with regard to taxes. You pay for attorneys' services by the hour.

- Financial Planner: Simply put, a financial planner helps you manage your finances. Whether you need a complete closet over-haul (budgeting, saving, taxes, investments, etc.) or just one perfect outfit (a specific goal, like help saving for a house), a financial planner can help you create a blueprint for any financial occasion. The way financial planners or investment advisors charge varies, so keep reading to learn more.

- Investment Advisor: Unlike financial planners, who focus on your whole life, these advisors focus specifically on your investment goals and plans. Investment advisors must be registered with either the Securities Exchange Commission or with state securities agencies before they can give you advice. They can help you find the classics (good investments) and avoid the trends (investments in favor at the moment, but that might not fit your needs, or that might be out of style and therefore lower in value in a short time). Yes, investments go in and out of style, too. You've heard of stock bubbles? When many investors flock to the same kind of investments, their price goes up higher than the underlying company fundamentals are worth. Eventually, as with all trends, people tire of them and move onto the next hot thing. When this happens, the stock price falls.

- Insurance Broker: These folks can help determine what kind of insurance you need and which policies and carriers would be best for you. Medical. Life. Car. Home. Renters'. They can also shop around for you to find the best deal among the various insurance companies. Their fees are paid by the insurance company. To you, they're free, although their salary and commissions are factored into the rates you pay.

- Realtor, a licensed professional who helps you find a home and navigates the home-buying process. Typically the person selling the home pays the costs of the realtor (both yours and theirs). But you need to make sure because sometimes sellers try to get the buyer to pay for some or all of their own agent's services.

- Stockbroker: Who doesn't want to be rich, fabulous, and well-dressed? The right stockbroker can make it happen. As we discussed, stocks are a good place to invest your money, especially when you are young. Stockbrokers help buy and sell securities products (stocks, bonds, mutual funds, indexes, etc.). But remember, you have to be able to handle the risk of potentially losing some, or even all, of your investment. Brokers must be registered with the National Association of Securities Dealers (NASD).

It's great to have a stylist and it's great to a have closet full of financial experts. However, you don't always need to have either one on hand. So before you run out and hire someone to help you with your finances, give it some thought. Maybe you are facing a specific life-changing event, like a wedding, a new child, a new job, a divorce, or an impending inheritance. Maybe you just have some specific financial goals you want help achieving. Once you have established that you need to hire someone, there are some things you should know.

I've mentioned before that financial professionals are paid in different ways. Some are **fee-based** meaning they charge either an hourly fee or a flat fee per project or they take a percentage of the total amount of money they manage for you. Others work on **commission**. They are paid to sell you financial products and they earn money from each product you buy. You should be careful of financial professionals who are paid solely on commission, since their self-interest can conflict with your best interests. Does "My dear, that looks fabulous on you, you just have to have it!" sound familiar? But commission-driven enthusiasm is easier to recognize in a store, especially if the mirror is telling you a different story. And, finally, some planners receive a combination of fees and commission. Before you hire anyone, be sure you ask how they are paid. If they receive commissions, know how much and on what products, so you can track their advice and determine who is benefiting most from it, them or you. Google them to review their credentials. Questions to ask prospective financial professionals include:

- "What credentials, licenses, and education do you have?" Be sure they have at least a four-year college degree and preferably an advanced degree in financial planning. Be sure they also have the appropriate registration and licenses. For example, an attorney will have a JD, and an accountant will almost always be a CPA, and a stockbroker will have a license.

- "What is your work experience? How long have you been in the business?" Be sure they have experience doing specifically what they are going to be doing for you—the more the better. You wouldn't hire a stylist who had never dressed anyone, and you don't hire a brand new person to help you pick your stocks.

- "Do you specialize in certain areas, services, or types of clients?" Some planners specialize just in investments; others in estate planning. Some require you to have a certain (high) net worth before they take you as a client. Find one who matches your needs.

- "Will you provide references?" Get references and contact them. See if they were happy with the service they got. Ask for current and past clients. Whether it's a stylist or a finance professional, word of mouth is always the best way to get information.

- "How are you paid?"

- "How will you help me implement my plans and achieve my goals?"

- "Will I deal directly with you or with an associate or both?" Some professionals work alone, others have lots of staff. If you are paying by the hour, working with a more junior person can save you money. You get the benefit of their boss's experience and judgment at a lower price.

Be sure you interview more than one advisor/planner to ensure you wind up with one that is on the same wave length as you. After all, if you dress punk, you don't want a stylist whose signature look is boho-chic.

. . .

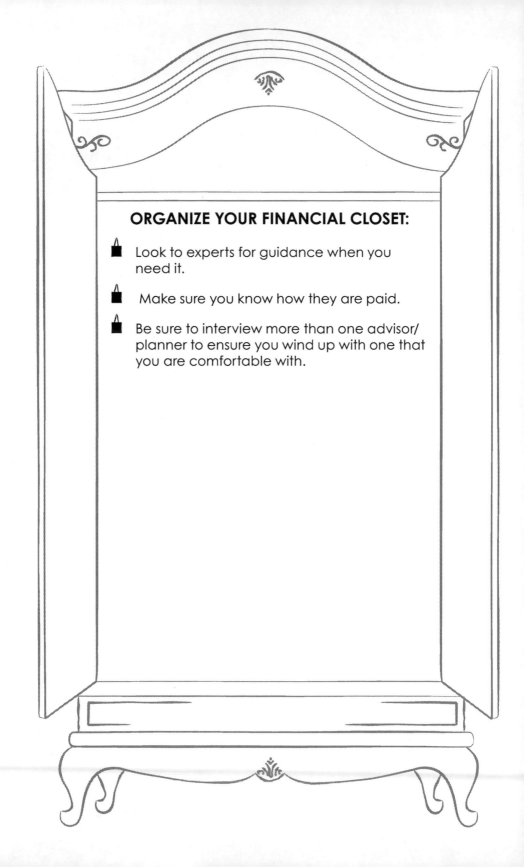

ORGANIZE YOUR FINANCIAL CLOSET:

- Look to experts for guidance when you need it.

- Make sure you know how they are paid.

- Be sure to interview more than one advisor/planner to ensure you wind up with one that you are comfortable with.

Conclusion

WALK THE RED CARPET

You were already a Fashionista. Now you can add **Financial Goddess** to your resume. But having shown you how to organize your financial closet, I would be remiss if I didn't help you organize your real one.

For a beautiful clothes closet, you should separate pants, dresses, skirts, and tops into their own sections. I recommend breaking suits up so you remember to wear the pieces as separates. If you are really advanced, organize each section by color, light to dark (black, grey, purple, blue, green, red, orange, pink, yellow, cream, and white). You can also put short-sleeve shirts first, then long, then blouses so they are separated. Sweaters should be folded; hanging them ruins their shape. Give away or donate anything that doesn't fit or you don't wear. By the way, I do not subscribe to the one-year rule—how long you should keep something. It depends on what it is. Designer pieces can live comfortably in your closet for many years. But if it hasn't seen the light of day for a long period of time, if it's stained, frayed, pilled, or otherwise not in good shape or hasn't fit since God knows when, it needs to go. Be ruthless. An organized closet makes getting dressed more fun and leaves you opportunities to fill in the gaps with more shopping—also fun.

Like an organized closet, organized finances are fun. Knowing what you have, what you don't have, and

what you need allows for a calmer, less stressful relationship with your money. Remember, with resolve, persever-
ance, and a sensible strategy, your coveted Chanel bag
is only a bit of financial planning away!

• • •

Glossary Of Terms

1. **Accountant:** A professional, who is usually but not always a CPA, who helps you maintain your financial records and prepares and submits your tax returns.

2. **Annual Percentage Rates (or APR):** Fees charged by credit card companies when you do not pay your bill in full.

3. **Appreciation:** The increase in value something has over time.

4. **Asset:** Anything you own that has commercial value.

5. **Asset allocation:** A reference to how you keep (or allocate) your money. It is a good idea to keep your extra money in a variety of places: Cash, stocks, bonds, houses, cars, etc.

6. **Attorney:** A practicing lawyer who provides overall legal advice and also sets up trusts, wills, and powers of attorney.

7. **Bond:** A loan to a company or to a government. When you buy a bond, you agree to loan your money to the company or government in exchange for interest payments they make to you and the return of your money at a later set date.

8. **Budget:** An itemized plan of what you earn and what you spend.

9. **Balancing (reconciling) your checkbook:** At the end of every month, you and the bank need to agree on the number of checks you wrote, their total dollar amount, the money you withdrew in addition to them from your ATM, and the deposits you made.

10. **Bank statement:** Each month your bank will send you a piece of paper that shows your ending balance from the last month, a list of all the checks you wrote, the deposits you made, and an ending balance for the current month.

11. **Broker:** A professional who can help you buy stocks, bonds, and mutual funds.

12. **Brokerage account:** An account held at a financial institution, like a bank, within which you can purchase and keep stocks, bonds, mutual funds, and other types of financial investments through a professional (called a broker).

13. **Capital gain:** The difference between what you paid for a stock or bond and what you sell it for. If the price for which you sold it is higher, you made money, and you pay a tax on that amount.

14. **Checkbook register:** The place in the front of your checkbook where you should write down all of the checks you have written and all of the deposits you have made.

15. **Checking account:** Provided by financial institutions so you have a place to deposit and withdraw your money.

16. **Claim:** The amount you ask your insurance company for after something you're insured against happens.

17. **Compound interest:** In which you are paid interest on your interest.

18. **Compounding period:** How frequently interest is charged, since it can be charged in yearly, monthly, weekly, and daily increments.

19. **Corporate taxes:** Taxes companies pay on their profits.

20. **Credit card:** A small but powerful piece of plastic. It allows you to buy something now, today, when you want it, and pay for it later.

21. **Credit score:** A number assigned to you that is, in effect, a snapshot of your credit risk at a particular point in time. Credit scores range from 350, which means you're a poor risk, to 850, which means you're a good risk.

22. **Credit agency:** A company that collects relevant information about you on behalf of lenders.

23. **Commission or commission rate:** Fees charged by brokers for their services.

24. **Credit limit:** The total amount the credit card company decides you can borrow on its credit card.

25. **Debt:** An amount of money that you owe.

26. **Debit card:** An extension of your checking or savings account. Each time you make a purchase, the money to pay for it is taken directly from either your checking account or your savings account, depending on which account you tell the bank to debit.

27. **Deductible:** The portion of the claim that you pay for, for which the insurance company is not responsible.

28. **Depreciation:** The loss in value any given possession has over time.

29. **Discount brokers:** A broker who gives you a discount on their commission for making stock or bond market trades for you in exchange for not giving you advice.

30. **Diversification:** Spreading your money among different types of investments.

31. **Excise taxes, also called "sin taxes":** Taxes levied on items like liquor, cigarettes and cigars, and gambling.

32. **Expenses:** All the money you spend, both practical and impractical.

33. **Fashionista:** An enthusiast of fashion.

34. **Federal Deposit Insurance Corporation (or FDIC):** Insurance provided by the government to protect you from losses of up to 250,000 dollars if your bank goes bankrupt.

35. **Federal income tax:** Pays for country-wide services like defense and education.

36. **Financial Goddess:** You.

37. **Financial planner:** A licensed professional who can help you manage your overall finances, not just your portfolio.

38. **Fixed interest rate:** In which the bank pays you (or you pay the bank) the same amount of interest each time a payment is made, based on a pre-agreed amount.

39. **401K:** A retirement plan offered by your employer. A 401K takes money out of your paycheck (you decide how much) and deposits it into a retirement savings account for you.

40. **Fund manager:** A licensed professional who manages mutual funds.

41. **Identity Theft:** When someone uses your personal information (like your name, Social Security number or credit card) without your permission to purchase things illegally in your name.

42. **Income:** Money you earn (bring in).

43. **Income tax form:** The form you file with the federal government, in which you report your income and the taxes you have already paid throughout the year.

44. **Index fund:** A type of mutual fund that is passively managed, meaning the fund seeks to mirror the market and there is no fund manager.

45. **Individual Retirement Account (or IRA):** A personal retirement account, different from a 401K, which is a company retirement account.

46. **Insurance:** When you make regular ongoing payments to an insurance company in order to protect yourself financially if something goes wrong.

47. **Insurance agents:** Professionals who help you determine what kind of insurance you need, how much of it you need, and which policies and carriers will work best for you.

48. **Interest:** Fees banks pay for the privilege of using your money or that you pay banks for the privilege of using their money (usually expressed as a percent).

49. **Interest rate:** The amount of those fees.

50. **Investment advisor:** A professional in giving investment advice who must be registered with the Securities Exchange Commission or state securities agencies.

51. **Impulse spending:** Spending without forethought—or much of any thought.

52. **Liability:** An obligation, something you owe. In insurance, a legal term for what your responsibility is to the other people involved.

53. **Local income tax:** Pays for town and city projects.

54. **Matching contribution:** An employer's contributions to your 401K account (usually a percentage of your paycheck up to a designated amount).

55. **Medicare:** Used by the federal government to aid people over sixty-five in paying for their medical care.

56. **Mutual fund:** Allows investors who have the same financial goals and objectives to pool their money together. As with a stock, you own a share, but of the fund, not of the individual company. Unlike a stock, a mutual fund can contain both stocks and bonds.

57. **Net worth:** The total of all of your assets minus the total of all of your liabilities.

58. **Opportunity cost:** What you will be giving up as a result of a decision you make.

59. **Outstanding deposits:** Any deposits you've made or fees you've earned that are not yet credited to your bank account.

60. **Outstanding withdrawals:** Any checks you've written or fees you've been charged that have not yet been subtracted from your bank account.

61. **Overdraft protection:** A bank will cover you for a short time if a check you've written does not immediately have the funds to pay for it in your bank account.

62. **Passbook savings account:** A basic savings account.

63. **Policy:** What you buy when you buy insurance, namely an insurance policy.

64. **Premium:** The amount you pay for an insurance policy.

65. **Prepaid card:** A debit card that has a specific amount of money paid into it by someone else, instead of being linked to a bank account.

66. **Principal:** The original amount of money you borrowed from a financial institution or charged on a credit card.

67. **Proof of loss:** What an insurance company requires you to provide in order to verify the claim you are making to it. Insurance companies won't just take your word that you need money.

68. **Property taxes:** Taxes on real estate (houses and land sometimes cars).

69. **Realtor:** A licensed professional who helps you find and navigate the home-buying process.

70. **Return on investment:** A measurement of how much your money has increased or decreased (gained or lost) relative to what you invested over a one-year time period.

71. **Risk:** The degree of probability that something will cause you to need your insurance company for financial assistance. Risk is also the amount of chance you are willing to take with your money when you purchase financial investments.

72. **Roth IRAs:** A type of personal retirement fund in which you pay taxes before funding it, thereby allowing the money you put into it to grow tax free.

73. **Sales tax:** Federal or state tax on stuff you buy.

74. **Savings account:** Provided by financial institutions to provide you with a safe place to save your money and earn interest. There are three kinds of such accounts: Basic, money market, and certificate of deposit (CD).

75. **Schedule C:** The section on an income tax form where you include income that did not come from a full-time employer.

76. **Simple interest:** When you borrow money, you pay back the amount you borrowed (principal) plus interest on it. The formula for calculating simple interest is: Interest equals Principal multiplied by Interest Rate multiplied by Time held.

77. **Social Security:** Funded by the deductions from your paycheck and used by the federal government to give financial assistance to people who are retired or disabled; the full name for Social Security is the Federal Insurance Contributions Act (FICA).

78. **Stock (share of stock):** Ownership in an individual company; how much ownership depends upon how much stock you buy.

79. **Stock market:** Where stocks, bonds, mutual and index funds are traded.

80. **Taxes:** Fees paid by everyone to help support federal, state, and local governments and their projects.

81. **Time value of money:** All things being equal, it is better to have money sooner rather than later.

82. **Variable interest rate:** The differing percentages of interest the bank pays you (or you pay the bank) based on how interest rates are performing at any given time; interest rates rise and fall depending on a variety of factors.

83. **W-2:** A tax form from your employer reporting your earnings and the amount of income tax they withdrew from your paycheck during the year.

84. **W-4:** A tax form requiring you to give your employer your permission to deduct taxes from your paycheck.

The Fashionistas Resource Guide

Here are some places you can go for additional help and inspiration:

1. *Sex and the City*—books, TV, and DVDs—I better not need to explain this one.

2. *Math Doesn't Suck* by Danica McKellar, www.math-doesntsuck.com. If you need a math refresher, I highly recommend this book. It is wickedly brilliant.

3. *The Money Book for the Young, Fabulous and Broke* by Suze Orman.

4. *The Smart Cookies' Guide to Making More Dough*, by the smart cookies with Jennifer Barrett, www.smartcookies.com.

5. www.about.com—for more information about how all of this personal finance works.

6. www.bluefly.com—for fashion at a discount.

7. www.cfp.net—Just as you would evaluate a stylist to see if their style works for you, you need to do the same with a financial planner. To find a financial planner that works for you, start with a Certified Financial Planner or find a Chartered Financial Analyst.

8. www.consumerreports.com—for homework and research on big-ticket items.

9. www.cosmopolitan.com—for fun and fashion (self explanatory).

10. www.consumercredit.com—for help finding a credit counselor.

11. www.dailycandy.com—for all things fun and fashionable.

12. www.elle.com – self explanatory.

13. www.fdic.gov—to see if a bank is federally insured.

14. www.ftc.gov—for identity theft prevention information and tips.

15. www.federalreserve.gov/Pubs/shop/—to help you select the right credit card.

16. www.google.com—so you can do your homework and research.

17. www.howstuffworks.com—for additional information on how all of this personal finance stuff works.

18. www.instyle.com—self explanatory.

19. www.kiplinger.com—for even more personal finance information.

20. www.luckymag.com—self explanatory.

21. www.morningstar.com—unbiased investment research.

22. www.net-a-porter.com—A great place to take a break but keep your credit card far away.

23. www.necal.bbb.org—for information on prepaid cards from the Better Business Bureau. There is also a good article on prepaid cards called *"The Pros and Cons of Prepaid Cards,"* which you can find

through Google. *The Wall Street Journal* also had a good article, *"The New Card On Campus: Pre-paid Debit,"* by Mary Pilon.

24. www.quicken.com, www.microsoftmoney.com, www.mint.com—computer programs to help you track everything automatically; plus they do budgets.

25. www.vogue.com—the bible.

26. www.rethinkrealestate.com —Tara-Nicholle Nelson's website for [Re]Thinking Real Estate.

27. www.wikihow.com—for tips on how to save, spend, invest, and budget.

28. www.wikipedia.org—for even more definitions and explanations.

• • •

Index

2611444

Made in the USA